Butterbox Survivors

Life After the Ideal Maternity Home

ROBERT HARTLEN

NIMBUS
PUBLISHING

Nimbus Publishing Limited
PO Box 9301, Station A
Halifax, NS   B3K 5N5
(902) 455-4286

Design: Margaret Issenman
Cover Captions: Rita McGurk and her adoptive parents, Rose and William Bendett. Bottom photo of children at the Ideal Maternity Home is dated 1944-45.

Printed and bound in Canada

Canadian Cataloguing in Publication Data
Hartlen, Robert, 1945-
Butterbox survivors
ISBN 1-55109-290-5
1. Adoptees—Canada—Biography.   2. Adoptees—United States—
Biography.   3. Adoption—Nova Scotia—Corrupt practices.
4. Ideal Maternity Home.   I. Title.

HV700.5.H37 1999   362.73'4'0922   C99-950024-4

Nimbus Publishing acknowledges the financial support of the Canada Council and the Department of Canadian Heritage.

To the memory of my parents:
Maude (Bartlen) Saulnier and Wilson Bartlen,
who chose and raised me with love,
and to Arthur Fulford and Violet Vennall,
who gave me the gift of life.
To my loving wife, Donna,
and my family, who have always been there for me,
and to all of the babies
of the Ideal Maternity Home
and their families.

Table of Contents

THE SONS SPEAK
— Canada —

— United States —

APPENDICES

Preface

THE IDEAL MATERNITY HOME 1928-1946

he Ideal Maternity Home was an idea conceived of in the hearts and minds of Lila and William Young. Lila Gladys (Coolen) Young was born in Fox Point, Nova Scotia. After finishing school, she became a teacher, and taught school in Fox Point. In 1925, at the age of 26, she met William Peach Young, her future husband. William was an un-ordained Seventh Day Adventist minister from Memramcook, New Brunswick. He graduated from the Medical Evangelists College in 1923, and was a self-designated medical missionary, caring for the sick and spreading the gospel along the South Shore of Nova Scotia.

Following their marriage, they moved to Chicago, and in December 1927, William graduated from the National College of Chiropractic. The same year, Lila graduated from the National School of Obstetrics and Midwifery. They returned to Nova Scotia, and in February 1928 opened "The Life and Health Sanitarium—Where the Sick Get Well." They worked out of their four-bedroom cottage in East Chester, with barely enough money to buy cots for the patients to sleep on. Lila started delivering babies, and within a year the Youngs were specializing in maternity services, largely for unwed mothers. Their business became known as the Ideal Maternity Home and Sanitarium.

For those seeking the services of the Ideal Maternity Home, privacy and discretion was guaranteed. Payment of between $100 and $500 on arrival was required, which provided for room and board, delivery, and arrangements for the adoption of the baby. There was an additional $12 for layette, and in the early days of operation, a babysitting service was available for an additional $2 per week. For those expectant mothers who were unable to pay the specified fees, arrangements could be made to work off the debt. This option made the services more readily available to impoverished unwed mothers looking for a safe place to have their babies. Often, these young mothers were entirely on their own, without support of family, friends, or the father of the unborn child. In

Dr. William Peach Young and Lila Young—founders of the Ideal Maternity Home.

cases where the baby didn't survive, there was also a $20 burial fee: $5 for a shroud, and $15 for the Youngs, who would be present at the burial. The Youngs provided a white pine "coffin," which was actually a butterbox from the LaHave Creamery, used to transport groceries to the Home. Lila described them as "white pine coffins, mitered and very smooth, and always lined with satin."

Detailed contracts were signed by the unwed mothers, giving William the power of attorney and legal authority over their babies and their babies' adoptions. If the mothers had not signed the contracts within fourteen days of the birth, they were charged an additional $30. By the time the girls were ready to leave the Home, their bills often exceeded $300. At that time, average wages for sales clerks were $8 per week, and for domestics, $4 per week.

As the Home became more widely known, through a rigorous advertising campaign by the Youngs, the number of babies for adoption increased. So did new markets fueled by the growing American tourist trade, opportunistic lawyers, and the greed of the Youngs. Many babies found new homes in the U.S.A., where state laws restricted many couples from adopting, due to their age, etc. These new parents were very grateful, and some made generous contributions to the Home. Although many children found good homes through these arrangements, they were not in all cases legal. In some instances, new parents were not aware that siblings (twins) had been separated to provide them with their chosen child, or that the child may have been taken away from its mother without her consent.

By the mid 1940s, pregnant girls coming to the Home were generating revenues of about $60,000 for the Youngs, but the real money was coming from the sale of babies. The fees charged for an adoption were between $1,000 and $10,000 each, depending on the financial ability of the adoptive parents. In addition, donations were requested and in many cases paid. Even allowing for babies that were not suitable for adoption, and for those who died—at least 10 per cent of the total—it is reasonable to estimate that half of the reported seven hundred or so babies sold over the eighteen years that the Home was in operation earned the Youngs about $5,000 each. That is a total of $3.5 million.

In 1933, the Youngs drew up elaborate plans to expand the Home. Renovations and expansions were completed in 1936, with William doing some of the work himself. In 1939, the Youngs paid off their mortgage on the Ideal Maternity Home, and then built another home—a three-storey house containing nine bedrooms, three bathrooms, a den, dining room, living room, and kitchen—for themselves and their five children. Over the next six years, they bought new cars, invested in land, and continued to add to their assets. By 1943, the Youngs had become wealthy. The cottage they had started with in 1928 was now a huge structure with fifty-four rooms and fourteen bathrooms. It had elegant turrets and was surrounded by expansive lawns and greenery, and most important to the Youngs, it was mortgage free.

By 1933, the provincial department of health had begun taking an interest in the Home. The Liberal Party swept into office that year, and Dr. Frank Roy Davis was appointed to the Public Health portfolio. Before long, he was introduced to problems at the Ideal Maternity Home. Questions about the medical training of the staff had been raised, and there had been gossip regarding unreported baby deaths. For the next fifteen years that he spent in office, Davis proved to be a thorn in the Youngs' booming baby business.

Early in 1936, the first evidence of criminal negligence at the Home was brought to the public's attention. A young woman, twenty-eight-year-old

Eva Neiforth, and her baby had both died in childbirth. On March 4, the Youngs were both arraigned on two counts of manslaughter. William was not officially charged, but Lila was committed for trial and confined to jail in Chester. She was released on $1,000 bail. Brought to trial in May of that year, Lila was found not guilty of the charges against her. Following this, Public Health Minister Frank Davis ordered the RCMP to investigate all known deaths at the Home. In the years that followed, Lila and William Young were under constant investigation. In 1939, they were charged with fraud by a father who had agreed, under contract, to pay the Youngs maintenance costs for his child until it had been adopted. The baby died in 1938, but the Youngs fraudulently continued to receive payments from the father until January 1939. They were again acquitted. The Youngs had built up a strong support group, which included prominent citizens and politicians. They presented themselves as upstanding members of the community who were providing a Christian service. If it looked as though things might go against them, they weren't above threatening significant people in society and politics who had discreetly used the services of the Home over the years. Until 1940, the Boarding House Act had not required that the Home have an operating license. But in 1940, the Maternity Boarding House Act was amended, and William and Lila were now required to apply for a license. They were turned down. On November 17, 1945, after five years of appeals and investigation, the Ideal Maternity Home was ordered closed.

Despite this, and because the Act lacked official support, the Youngs continued to operate their business and to advertise "Lovely Babies for Adoption." Frank Davis looked for new ways to close the Ideal Maternity Home forever, beginning with tracking adoptions. New Jersey officials were anxious to cooperate, as they were also trying to crack down on illegal adoptions and baby smuggling. In the fall of 1945, a New Jersey newspaper reported that a child-smuggling scheme between Canada and the U.S. had been uncovered. To avoid fueling an even bigger scandal, child welfare officials in Canada and the U.S. clamped down on the unauthorized movement of adopted babies across borders. But by now, the Youngs were old hands at circumventing the law. They simply arranged for the birth mothers to travel with their babies to the U.S. Finally, however, after numerous charges, court appearances, and fines, the Youngs closed their maternity home and re-opened the facility as a hotel. About the same time, a Montreal newspaper published an article by Mavis Gallant about the Youngs' maternity business, bringing it under heavy scrutiny from both Canadian and U.S. law agencies. The Youngs sued the newspaper for slander, but lost their case.

Following the trial, the Youngs developed serious financial problems, business dropped, their profits dwindled, and they were now in debt. Bankrupt, they left East Chester as penniless as they were when they arrived thirty years earlier.

The hotel was eventually taken over by Edward Corkum of Robinson's Corner and later fell to his son, Roy, who eventually sold it to a Mr. G. Crooks. On September 23, 1962, fire broke out in the building, which was in the process of being converted into apartments, burning it to the ground, despite the efforts of the Chester Fire Department.

Several years after their departure, William died of cancer, and Lila returned to Nova Scotia to resume teaching near Fox Point. In 1969, at the age of 70, Lila died of leukemia and was buried in the Seventh Day Adventist Cemetery in Fox Point—close to the many babies, in their butterbox coffins, who didn't have a chance to enjoy life.

The Ideal Maternity Home. The original dwelling and other buildings were gradually replaced by this "well-equipped modern institution."

Prologue

They took in all the young girls
whose bellies swelled with shame,
delivered them a girl or boy
by some fictitious name.

And in their vicious kindness
they left the sick to die,
but fed the cute and healthy ones
for friend or foe to buy.

The ones who died were carted off
to a furnace or the sea,
or buried in a butterbox
in shrouds of secrecy.

And we the ones who brought a fee
we search for who we are,
aside from one or two of us
we've had no luck so far.

No matter where we're going
we don't know where we've been,
we don't know where we're coming from
whose family tree we're in.

We look up to the stars at night
and know they're looking down,
on someone else who's looking up
from some strange nameless town.

They say that we're the lucky ones
the ones who brought a fee,
but till we find that butterbox
we never will be free.

Janice L. Street

A few of the older babies. Publicity photo from the Ideal Maternity Home and Sanitarium Ltd., East Chester, N.S.

More of the older babies of the Ideal Maternity Home (approx. 1944/1945).

Foreword

utterbox Survivors is a collection of personal stories as told by some of the Survivors of the Ideal Maternity Home, by the parents who chose them, and by the mothers who gave birth to them. Many issues related to the Home are touched on, as are issues related to adoption in general.

Both birth mothers and adoptive parents describe conditions at the Ideal Maternity Home, and their stories are fairly consistent. They tell of choosing a baby as if shopping in a supermarket, especially in the early to mid 1940s. By all reports, there were anywhere from thirty-five to one hundred or more babies to choose from. The home advertised healthy babies, yet these parents recall that a surprising number of babies were actually ill or showing signs of neglect at the time they were chosen. There are stories of mothers being told that their babies had died at birth or shortly thereafter, only to discover many years later that their children did survive, and were sold to well-to-do families. Years later, several of these "babies" were reunited with their birth mothers. Some mothers speak of the unpleasant conditions at the Home, while others remember it as a good place to have been.

Of course, the stories presented provide only a partial view of what went on at the Ideal Maternity Home. No one knows for sure how many babies actually passed through the Home, or where they ended up. We know that many were adopted or placed with families in the United States, while others remained in Canada. In some cases, babies were given free to families who were willing to care for them and give them a home, while the adoption of others involved payments or fees, some amounting to $10,000, or more. Some of the issues that have plagued many of the Survivors are related to religious and racial issues. In some cases, requests by the birth mothers to have their child placed with families of the same religion were honoured, but in many other cases they were ignored. "Placing" the children was the priority. Many grew up feeling that they were living outside their culture, without knowing why. Growing up and feeling "different" created many difficulties for the children that they did not confront until they reached adulthood, when the need to understand who they were intensified. Many never knew they were adopted until late in life. Victims of the secrecy surrounding their birth, they had to face the sad realization that their life, as they knew it, had all been a lie. For some, the greatest shock was learning the history of the Ideal Maternity Home—the stories of babies who didn't survive, or of those reportedly starved to death on a diet of molasses and water, and of those buried in unmarked graves in various locations around the county. The stories of babies being unceremoniously dumped at sea or disposed of in the furnaces of the Home were to become the nightmares that haunted many of the adult Survivors. They have been living in the shadows of lies, deceit, secrecy, and a bureaucratic system that reinforces all three. Now they live under another shadow—the shadow of the butterbox. Except for an unpredictable fate, they too could have been among the children who did not survive.

The Birth
of a Support Group

ollowing the closure of the Ideal Maternity Home in August 1946, life in the village of East Chester continued its daily routine, and eventually the Home became just a memory. Many people would have preferred that it stayed that way, but it wasn't to be. As a new generation grew into adulthood, the subject of the Ideal Maternity Home re-surfaced. As adults, many people were discovering that they had been adopted, and with this discovery new questions were being asked. Some did find out from their adoptive parents, or by accessing documents long secreted away, that they had been born at the Ideal Maternity Home. For many, the name "Ideal" was comforting, and they had very little reason to discuss their place of birth, knowing that many young expectant mothers chose to go to maternity homes to have their babies.

It wasn't until 1988, when a local reporter, Bette Cahill, began investigating baby deaths and other scandals surrounding the Home, that "survivors" became involved. Although many local residents chose not to discuss the past, there were others who told what they remembered, and the story burst wide open again, almost fifty years later. Several people who knew of their birth connection with the Home made contact with reporters and eventually with each other. Shocked by what they were hearing, they had many questions, but received few answers. Some adoptees who grew up in the local community had never heard of the stories now being discussed, though they remembered both the Home, and Lila and William Young from when they were children. With the 1992 publication of Cahill's *Butterbox Babies*, survivors of the Ideal Maternity Home sought out each other. As they came together and shared their memories of the Home, they were horrified. They realized that they were lucky to be alive, and were grateful to their adoptive families, without whom they may not have survived the horrors described in Cahill's book. Some ended up with loving and devoted families; others were not so fortunate. As they came together, the "Survivors," as they referred to themselves, realized that they had a story to tell.

Following the publication of *Butterbox Babies*, a play by the same name was written, and then performed at various places around Nova Scotia. In August 1992, the movie *Butterbox Babies* was produced by Sullivan Films, and has since been shown all over North America. In 1997, another play about the Ideal Maternity Home, entitled *Aftermath*, was developed out of new stories from the Survivors. It was performed for the Survivors and Friends of the Ideal Maternity Home, at an international reunion of the Home's Survivors.

Through the efforts of many people, but particularly Michael Reider, who was living in Ontario at the time, a support group was born, and information and friendship shared. As the Survivors came into contact with each other, a bond—almost like a "birth bond"—was created. Social barriers dropped, and everyone supported each other in a quest for answers. Michael and his wife, Norma, published a newsletter entitled "The Search," which they circulated, and the group began to grow. As they grappled with their birth history, many of that original group felt that a memorial service would be appropriate to honour and remember the many babies of the Home who didn't survive and who, for the most part, had been forgotten by history. With the help and support of other Survivors of the Home, the dream of a memorial service became a reality and information about it was sent out across the country via the newsletter.

On Friday, November 27, 1992, at 11 A.M., the first memorial service for the babies who died at the Home, and for the Survivors of the Ideal Maternity Home, was held in the small village of Chester, Nova Scotia.

St. Stephen's is a beautiful church, old and regal, bright and welcoming, that stands on a hill overlooking Chester. It was a fitting location for the ceremony. In the bright morning sun, the story of the Butterbox

Babies, hidden from so many for so long, was brought into the light. Not just the "light" of news broadcasts, books, or newspapers, but the "light" of people who were part of the story, worshipping together where it had all taken place. Each had a different reason for being there, but there was a singleness of purpose.

A public memorial service, long overdue, was also held. There were tears mixed with smiles at this bittersweet union and reunion of people trying to make sense of the time lost to a clouded and veiled past.

The heavens did not fall, and Lunenburg County was not swept out to sea in a tidal wave of shame or anger, as some had predicted. The Survivors felt they had the right to be there, and did what they knew to be appropriate and timely for themselves, and for the memory of those who had died.

St. Stephen's was nearly full, and people greeted each other as brothers and sisters separated by time and distance. The congregation was made up mainly of Survivors and their families, a few local residents, and the media. Although each person had their own thoughts and feelings, most Survivors realized that they could have been one of the unfortunate children who didn't survive.

Reverend Ed Tuck of St. Stephen's gave the opening remarks and welcome, while Reverend Andy Crowell, representing the Lunenburg County Ecumenical Fellowship, conducted the liturgical service of readings, hymns, and prayers. Following the liturgy, a tape of a song written by Norma Reider was played. Norma, an accomplished pianist, had composed many pieces over the previous few years that were inspired by the Survivors' personal searches and the unfolding story of the Butterbox Babies. The congregation followed the lyrics to the song, which were printed in the Order of Service. Then Michael Reider attempted to answer the question, "Why are we here today?" His response to that question reflected the feelings of everyone in the church that day, as they sat motionless, in silence, except when brushing away their tears.

Why Are We Here Today?

"We are here today to remember those who are not here.
They are not here because many years ago they died;
Some were left to die, some were made to die.
They were our brothers and sisters,
They were our sons and daughters.
They were the children of our nation.
We come together in this House because it is a visible token of
the presence of God.
Its beauty is the beauty of Holiness; the Church as champion of
justice, mercy, and peace.
As it is written, "My house shall be called a house of prayer for
all peoples."
Today, here, we come not as Jew or Gentile, Catholic or
Protestant,
We come here as mourners and we mourn as one.
We mourn for the lives never lived,
For teachers who never taught,
For nurses who never healed,
For lovers who never loved,
For dreamers who never dreamed.
We mourn them, each and every one,
Even though we know the names of only a few.
Each name is precious, each name a prayer so solemn,
So holy it is known only to God.
Their birth was a secret.
Their life was a secret.
Their slow starvation was a secret.
Their suffering was a secret.
Their death was a secret.
Even their burial place was a secret.
For forty-five and more years the secret has been whispered.
It is time now to end the secrecy and remember the dead as the
dead should be remembered,
With honour, and with respect.

*I pray that the horror of the story that has come to be known
as the "Butterbox Babies" never overshadows the most
important of truths.*

That the Butterbox Babies were real.

As real as my children and your children,

*As real as the children we see in the arms of moms and dads
each day.*

They lived, they smiled, they cried,

And they breathed this Nova Scotia air.

*But when they no longer had monetary potential they become a
burden.*

No one wanted these babies.

There was no one to protect these babies.

There were few who even knew of these babies.

*And so, in this thick veil of secrecy and apathy, they were
victimized.*

They were the ones that were left behind.

*And, how many of us can say, "There, but for the Grace of God,
Would I be."*

Each of us enters this sanctuary with a similar purpose,

*Yet each of us arrives with his or her own needs that we lay
before God.*

Some bring hearts full of gratitude.

They may be the Survivors of the Home who, like myself,

Have been reunited with their natural families

*And have found love and acceptance with their new-found
mothers and fathers,*

Sisters and brothers.

Let us rejoice in their happiness.

Some enter this sanctuary bringing hearts aching with sorrow.

*Disappointments weigh heavily upon them and they have
known despair.*

*Their search for that one vital connection that would make life
seem complete proves fruitless.*

Among us today are children looking for parents

And parents looking for children

And siblings searching for sibling.
Let us encourage them and support them in their quest.
Some have entered this house with hearts embittered.
They have sought answers in vain.
Life has lost meaning and value.
They seek revenge when none is possible.
May the knowledge that we too are searching for meaning in all
*   that has happened,*
Restore their hope and give them courage to believe that all is
*   not emptiness.*
Allow us to open our hearts to God and to one another.
Some come today with spirits that hunger.
They long for a friendly smile.
They crave understanding.
They question their own actions back then.
They live with "if only" and "what if I had."
Many years ago was just that—many years ago.
We cannot undo the past.
We can only work to see what went wrong then,
And striving, gain strength from one another.
And, as we share our joys and our sorrows,
Our successes and our regrets,
Lighten each other's burdens."

Following the service, thirteen cars drove the thirty-five miles to a burial site adjacent to the Seventh Day Adventist Cemetery. It was an unpleasant experience for most. The area was, and still is completely overgrown and almost inaccessible. Several people walked to the grave sight of Lila Young, located only a few steps from the pathway leading to the resting places of the Butterbox Babies.

* * *

The Survivors Group was fairly inactive over the next few years, with infrequent contact between members. Fortunately, some members had maintained contact with each other, which facilitated bringing the group back into an active state. Although everyone thought it would be a great idea to remain in contact, and missed the news about each other, everyone was also too busy to take on the responsibility. Mike couldn't do it alone. I had been one of the members of the group who maintained contact with several people whom I met at the memorial service. In the fall of 1996, I decided to take a more active role on behalf of the group. Not knowing where to start, I contacted Mike Reider and told him that I was ready to give him some of the help that he had been asking for. Mike sent me mailing lists and relevant information concerning the group. In the meantime, I invested in another computer, and painstakingly went through the motions of producing a newsletter. With the help of many friends, I also established a web site dedicated to the Ideal Maternity Home (Home of the Butterbox Babies). With access to the Internet, I subscribed to some of the other adoption groups in both Canada and the United States, looking for and sharing information. A whole new communication network was established, and before long, many new Survivors of the Ideal Maternity Home started to make contact.

In January 1997, a small committee made up of Survivors living in the Halifax metro area met as part of the regular monthly meeting of Parent Finders Nova Scotia. As a result of this meeting, plans started to be made for a second memorial service, to be held in the late summer or early fall of 1997. This meeting marked the birth of the Search and Support group, which became known as the Survivors and Friends of the Ideal Maternity Home. The group continues to grow, with members from all across Canada, the U.S., and Europe. Not only do we have the support of the Survivors, but we also have the support of Parent Finders, which has proven to be the most valuable of our resources, resulting in several reunions for members of our group.

The Survivors and Friends of the Ideal Maternity Home was officially incorporated as a non-profit group under the Societies Act on March 12, 1997, after a successful application for this status to the Registrar of Joint Stocks. Shortly after this, a date was set for a second memorial service, and plans were made to establish a monument, which would be dedicated to all of the babies of the Ideal Maternity Home. By this time, the newsletter was being published again and the information was circulated to the members of the group.

It was hoped that the service could have been held at St. Stephen's

Anglican Church, the site of the 1992 Memorial, but that wasn't possible. After making several contacts in the community, the Chester Baptist Church agreed that the service could take place at their church, and Reverend Dan Green of Chester agreed to officiate. It was hoped that the monument might be secured and ready for dedication at the same time.

Applications for funding and grants were submitted, without favourable response from the government, so a fundraising campaign was organized. Immediately, donations from Survivors all over the continent started to arrive, as well as offers of assistance. A variety of suggestions regarding the monument were investigated and finally a decision was made to commission Greg DeMone of DeMone Monuments in Lunenburg. Greg worked in consultation with the group and incorporated the ideas submitted, resulting in a beautiful piece of art, which now stands proudly in front of the East Chester Recreation Centre, next to the property on which the Ideal Maternity Home originally stood.

In addition to the many donations sent by the Survivors to fund the monument and the weekend activities, the major part of the fundraising campaign came about with the writing of *Aftermath*. The idea was conceived by John Brown and I, as a unique way of telling the story of the Ideal Maternity Home, but from the Survivors' memories, rather than basing it on the original story, *Butterbox Babies*. John, who is a writer, producer, director, and actor (in addition to his regular employment) was willing to undertake the project, but said that we should "try for the best first," and approached another friend—talented writer, director, and actress Flo Trillo. After reviewing copies of stories and archival material, Flo agreed to write the play. Things progressed fairly quickly. The play was written, the cast chosen, rehearsals started, and enthusiasm built, as the date of the memorial weekend got closer. The Chester Playhouse Theatre agreed to three performances, one of which was a benefit performance.

During this time, press releases were sent out across North America, and stories about the Ideal Maternity Home, the Survivors, and the memorial weekend began appearing everywhere. As the stories surfaced, so did new Survivors, some finding out for the first time their connection with the infamous Ideal Maternity Home, and more importantly, with other people, who had shared "their" experience. As Survivors contacted each other, bonds were created, and we were all looking forward to meeting together in Chester.

When I thought about bringing the group back into an active state, I never dreamed that things would or could happen so quickly. The reunion, memorial service, and monument dedication hosted by and for the Survivors and Friends of the Ideal Maternity Home, held during the weekend of August 29–31, was a huge success.

Survivors and their families came from all over North America, including Florida, Colorado, Arizona, Texas, Maine, Massachusetts, New Jersey, New York, and Ontario, New Brunswick, and Nova Scotia. On Sunday, more than four hundred people filed into the Chester United Baptist Church to participate in the memorial service, and then made the short pilgrimage to East Chester where the monument was dedicated to all the babies of the Ideal Maternity Home.

The weekend began with an informal reception that my wife, Donna, and I hosted at our home in Halifax. More than seventy people shared in the opening night of the weekend, most meeting in person for the first time. Immediately the bonds of friendship and a sense of belonging were formed, and stories and memorabilia were exchanged. In addition to the Survivors and their families, the local and national media were also in attendance and began documenting this memorable and historic weekend.

On Saturday, the gathering merged in the village of Chester and surrounding area, many returning there for the first time since leaving as infants so many years ago. The abundance of white ribbons worn by the Survivors was evident as people explored the village and the shops. A large number of the group met at the Windjammer Restaurant to share their evening meal and fellowship before venturing on to the Chester Playhouse to attend the benefit performance of *Aftermath*. The restaurant was bursting with activity, laughter, photo flashes, hugs and memory-book signings. There were no strangers there, only old friends finally being reunited. Already this event had become more than a Survivors' reunion; it had become a "family reunion." As the meal ended, the excitement continued to build as people started for the Chester Playhouse Theatre.

Needless to say, the performance—even with extra seats—was sold out. There were feelings of excitement, anticipation, and anxiety over what the show would be like. After all, this was the Survivors' story, and there would be something that would touch home for everyone, whether their particular story was portrayed or not. The cast was ready, though in some cases feeling a bit intimidated. They were presenting real-life stories and some of the characters being portrayed were in the audience. Before the play, I had the honour of addressing the audience. It was awesome—and a real test in emotional control— to look into the faces of so many people with whom I shared a common bond; I could think of no place I would rather have been.

For the next hour and a half, the audience was totally captivated by the performance. There was laughter, tears, and a tremendous feeling of togetherness in the theatre. Following a superb performance and a standing ovation, the audience and cast moved to the lobby for a reception. Again, words of thanks were expressed, hugs exchanged, and tears wiped, as tokens of appreciation were presented to the cast, crew, director/author, and producer. The crowd filled both the lobby and the street in front of the theatre.

On Sunday, amid sunny skies, the crowd assembled again, this time at the Baptist Church in Chester, for the memorial service. Reverend Dan Green and I gave the opening address, then a poem written for the occasion was read by Kathleen Benedict, which was followed by another reading by Rose Neil. Helen Irwin of New Jersey read the Scripture, and the message of hope was presented by Sharon Knight of Arizona and her family. A service for the Survivors, by the Survivors.

Following the memorial service, the congregation moved on to East Chester, where a short ceremony was held and where I, along with Ilene Steinhauer of New Jersey, had the honour of dedicating and unveiling the monument for the babies of the Ideal Maternity Home. Ilene and I were born at the Home on the same day—June 22, 1945. She was adopted by a family from the United States, and I by a family here in Nova Scotia. Although in contact for the past several months via e-mail, we were reunited in person on the site where our lives began. I am sure that back in 1945, none of the people at the Ideal Maternity Home could ever have envisioned such an event as was taking place not more than one hundred feet from where the Home stood.

Following the dedication of the monument and many floral tributes, the Survivors went to the actual site of the Ideal Maternity Home and had a group photo taken to mark the historic occasion. We rejoiced that we were there on the spot in friendship. Some discreetly picked up small fragments from the foundation of the Home, as a tangible reminder of that day, and took them home to sit beside other mementos, including, for some, fragments of the Berlin Wall, and of the empty concentration camps made famous during the Holocaust in Europe—all symbols of inhumanity.

At the end of a very busy and emotional day, there was one final thing to do. One of the floral tributes was removed from the monument, and a group of Survivors and friends made the trip to Fox Point, where tribute was paid, and prayers said again for the many babies buried randomly amid the tangled alder bushes adjacent to the Seventh Day Adventist Cemetery. As we stood looking into that maize of alders, it was hard to imagine that this could be a final resting place for anyone, let alone so many innocent babies, who never had a chance to live their lives. A place so desolate and out of sight, but no longer out of mind.

Survivors on the site of the Ideal Maternity Home, August 1997.

THE MOTHERS SPEAK

A Mother's Love
– and Anguish

VIOLET EISENHAUER

O n Friday morning, December 19, 1997, under clear, crisp, winter skies, a procession of nine cars slowly made its way through the tiny village of Chester Basin, Nova Scotia. The group was in search of answers, and possibly a conclusion, to a fifty-seven-year-old mystery—what really happened to Faith Lu Tanya Eisenhauer? The majority of the group were members of the press and television media, who were following a story and hoping to witness the event that would answer that question once and for all. There were several Survivors of the infamous Ideal Maternity Home—the "refuge" where Faith Lu Tanya's mother last saw her child alive. Mrs. Violet Eisenhauer, Faith Lu's anxious mother, believed that the baby she had been told years ago was buried in a satin-lined butterbox, was still alive. Violet's thoughts drifted back almost fifty-seven years, to the time when she, a twenty-year-old wife, and her husband were anticipating the birth of their first child. Living in the community of Chester Basin, only miles from the Ideal Maternity Home, Violet chose to have her child there, rather than in the Grace Maternity Hospital in Halifax, some sixty miles away. The Home, after all, offered obstetrical services, under the capable direction of Lila Young, whom Violet believed to be a qualified doctor. When Violet's husband, Stirling, objected, she assured him that there was no need to travel all the way to Halifax.

2

As Violet neared the cemetery, she was filled with both apprehension and hope. Finally she would know if her infant daughter was in the tiny grave at the corner of the Eisenhauer family cemetery plot, or if she was alive somewhere, the daughter of adoptive parents. Violet had never been convinced that Faith Lu Tanya had died. The circumstances surrounding the death and burial of her baby were too bizarre. Earlier, when being interviewed by a local journalist, Violet had insisted that, "None of us saw the dead baby, none of us. She [Mrs. Young] said, 'Never mind the burial, I'll take care of it.' What doctor would say that? But I was too sick to protest. I believed her. It never crossed my mind until a few years ago when the media started up again. Then I heard about other girls who were told their children died. They grew up and some of them found their mothers. All this got in my head and I thought, maybe my daughter is alive too."

Although a difficult decision to make, the only way to know for sure was to exhume the tiny grave that held the answer to the questions that had plagued Violet and her family throughout the years. When the cars arrived at the Lakeview Baptist Cemetery, Violet, dressed warmly in her black coat and fur-trimmed hat, stayed in the car with supportive friends to wait through this, the final vigil. Lying in bed, seriously ill and sedated at the time of her baby's death, neither Violet nor her family were allowed to see the dead child. As she looked across the cemetery, where the coffin would soon be exposed, she said with determination in her voice, "I wasn't here when they put her in the ground, but I am here today. I hope they don't find her...I hope she isn't there." As the day passed slowly, Violet occasionally walked to the grave to check the progress, then returned to the car, hoping, praying, and perhaps shedding the occasional tear for the tiny infant she nursed and held so dear, fifty-seven years ago.

Violet Eisenhauer was only one of between 1,000 and 1,500 young mothers to choose the Ideal Maternity Home during the years it operated—1928 to 1946. Unmarried expectant mothers came from all over Canada to have their babies in a "safe and discreet environment," away from what Lila Young referred to in her advertising brochures as "Dame Gossip." For a fee, payable in advance, and the assigning of power of attorney over to Dr. and Mrs. Young for the care and placement of the baby, a young woman could have her child in secrecy, arrange for its adoption, and often return home with no one ever knowing. But in addition to the unwed mothers who went to the Home, many married women from the local community took advantage of having the services of such a qualified couple as the Youngs, and had their children there as well. The married women usually stayed in the main house—the Youngs' private residence—whereas the other girls stayed in the main hospital.

Violet had known about the Ideal Maternity Home since she was a child. Although she knew that many local women went there to have their babies, she remembers that older people in the community were reluctant to talk about the Home. Violet had dreamed of becoming a writer, but before her career flowered, she met and married Sterling Eisenhauer in 1939. The young couple moved into her mother's home, and shortly after, Sterling joined the army and was stationed to Halifax, where he became an infantry cook. Violet remained in Chester Basin. Shortly after, Violet discovered that she was pregnant with their first child. As time drew closer to her delivery date, she decided, over her family's objections, to have her baby close to home, at the Ideal Maternity Home. As she remembers, "I wasn't really excited, only a bit afraid of the unknown. The home was close and Mrs. Young was a good doctor, and I felt safe. I told my husband that I was having this baby, not him. It wasn't till later that I found out, too late, that she wasn't a doctor. This was a big mistake."

On July 6, 1940, Violet went into labour, and was rushed to the Home. Violet's father was so nervous he could hardly do a thing. Violet was taken into the Youngs' home and settled into a small bedroom. After twelve hours, she started having regular contractions. As the pain got worse, Violet knew that something was wrong. The pain increased over the next few hours, and Violet was sure that she and the baby were going to die. It was then that she realized that Lila wasn't a doctor, or even a nurse. Lila told her that the umbilical cord was wrapped around the baby's neck, and that the baby was in trouble, but she wasn't sure what to do. Violet screamed that the baby was coming out backwards, and Lila panicked. There were no nurses in the house—they were all next door in the main hospital. "Lila kneeled down beside the bed and started to pray and to cry, praying for God to help save my life," Violet recalls.

Although weak, and sure she was dying, Violet managed to call out to one of the girls in the next room to telephone her doctor, Dr. Zwicker in Chester. Lila, who regained her composure, stopped the girl before she could make the call. "I'm still in charge here and you can't call the doctor," she asserted.

Fortunately, Dr. Young arrived just then. Violet was relieved, knowing that he was a doctor. He took over and delivered the baby safely. It was a breech birth, and a difficult one, but the baby was all right. Dr. Young stayed up all that night with her, afraid that she might bleed to death. Despite everything, Violet became the proud mother of a beautiful eight-and-one-half-pound baby girl, whom she named Faith Lu Tanya. Speaking of the birth later, Violet said, "[Dr. Young] was a good doctor as far as I'm concerned. He saved my life."

Violet had already chosen a name for her baby before coming to the Home, but two of her housemates, Faith and Tanya, asked to have the baby named for them. Violet had only just met them, but named the baby after them anyway. Violet didn't think the two names went together, so she added "Lu" in the middle. She said that the Lord knows the name of an unborn child, and this was the name hers was meant to have.

For the next two weeks, Violet nursed her baby, and her parents visited every day, but Sterling couldn't leave Halifax. Baby Faith thrived, but Violet's health worsened. She felt nauseated, and couldn't eat without being physically sick, because of abdominal infection. During this time, Lila cared for Violet, encouraging her to eat, and placing large hot lights over her abdomen to help the healing process. Despite being burned from the intense heat of the lamps, Violet felt comfortable under Lila's care.

While confined to bed, Violet had the opportunity to meet and become friends with some of the girls at the Home. "I met many girls in 1940—some I forget, but that place was always full of girls who were expecting. There was a girl named Jenny, who had a baby girl the day after mine, on July 8, 1940. I remember others; a girl from Cape Breton called Peggy, who had a baby boy, and Betty Ann, a wealthy girl, dark and beautiful, from Montreal. I learned later that her real name was Ruth Reid, and she had a baby girl. Another, Molly Swinnamer, had a baby boy, who was also placed for adoption. Molly, whose married name was Hiltz, died several years ago with cancer. Faith had a boy, as did Tanya." Violet enjoyed their friendship, but never heard from them after they left the Home.

Being married, she was respected by the other girls, and some of them came to ask her advice, or to tell her their own stories and troubles. Many couldn't afford to pay the fees charged by the Youngs, so agreed to work off the cost of their stay and for the care of their babies. The Home was a busy place, and there was lots of work to be done: clothes needed to be washed and ironed, floors scrubbed, food cooked, dishes done, and of course the babies needed to be cared for. Some of the girls found the work hard, but they had to do it to pay the bills.

Violet remembers a fair-haired, blue-eyed girl from Yarmouth. She was close to having her baby and was finding the chores harder to keep up with. She went by the name Virginia, but Violet didn't know if it was her real name or not. Most of the girls there didn't use their real names. Violet and Virginia became very close friends. Virginia had a baby boy in August or September, and named him Larry.

Violet also recalls that while she was bedridden, a child named Eva, who was about nine months old, "…had fallen down the stairs while they were having church over in the other place. When they returned to the house, they found her lying at the foot of the stairs, dead. Her mother had been 'boarding' her at the Home and planned to claim her one day. All I could hear was the child bumping and crying. Jenny was there also, but we were in the place alone and couldn't get out of bed. I wonder what they told the mother of little Eva. She would have been born in 1939."

One day, Virginia told Violet that there were some people from Winnipeg visiting the Home who wanted to adopt Faith. They insisted that they wanted a baby girl, but apart from Faith, there were no other girls in the nursery. Violet said that she didn't worry about it, because she was married, and the Youngs knew that she and Sterling were keeping their child. That was clearly understood from the very beginning. The next day, that same couple returned to the Home. This time Virginia listened at the keyhole while they were talking with the Youngs in the office. She clearly heard Lila say, "This baby was born in wedlock and can't be adopted." She also heard the couple reply, "Can't you pull some strings?" Virginia couldn't hear the rest of the conversation.

Then came the night that Violet will never forget. Lila came to her room on the evening of July 20, 1940, carrying a baby in her arms. The baby looked pale and sick. Lila cradled the baby in her arms and told Violet that her baby was ill. The baby looked bigger and older than Faith, but Lila was standing on the far side of the room in the shadows. Violet thought it was odd that Lila wouldn't bring Faith closer. She decided that this wasn't her baby; she knew that her baby was healthy, because she had nursed her.

The next morning, fourteen days after Faith was born, Violet was ready to go home; her husband and her father were coming to pick her up. Just before they arrived, Lila came to her bedside and told her that the baby had taken a fit through the night and had died. Still weak and unable to walk, Violet pleaded on deaf ears to see her baby, but Lila insisted, "You're too ill, you're not in any condition to see the baby," and helped her lie back on the bed. When Violet's family arrived, Lila told them that the baby was not fit to be seen; that it had turned black.

"I don't remember too much about that time," Violet says, "I was pretty sick and I was sedated, and the next thing I knew I was home. My mother had knitted a pretty pink dress for Faith, and she wanted it put on her for the funeral. Lila told her that the dress was gone, that she gave it to a baby girl who had been adopted the previous day. My husband made the funeral arrangements with the Youngs. He paid them $75 and then they wanted more money for a casket. On the day of the funeral, the Youngs brought the casket, a butterbox, to my mother's house. My father still wanted to see the baby, but Lila still wouldn't let him. The top was screwed shut, and Lila explained again that the baby had turned black. My father shouted that he didn't care if the baby was black as tar, he wanted to see her, but Lila still calmly said, 'I'm sorry Mr. Hatt, I'm not going to open that casket.'

"Lila took the casket to the Lakeview Baptist Cemetery in Chester Basin and it was buried in the Eisenhauer family plot, and not at the Fox Point site, where a lot of the babies were buried. It was buried under a birch tree and the Youngs stayed until every last shovelful of dirt was thrown into the tiny grave and remained there until every family member was gone."

Violet's father was still determined to see the body of the baby, so that night he and Sterling planned to go back to the cemetery and dig up the grave to see for themselves what was in the box. Violet's mother became upset, and talked them out of it. Violet says, "I wish that she would have let them go; then we would have known for sure if my baby was there or not. I don't think there was anything in that box. I think they stole my baby and sold her. I can't prove it, but I truly believe that's what happened. My mother wouldn't let us go to the law either, so we just kept it to ourselves. I was pretty depressed when all of this happened, and then I got really sick again and had to go to the hospital in Halifax, where they finally cured the abdominal infection."

Violet Eisenhauer at the Memorial/ Reunion—August 31, 1997.

When she recovered and returned home, she spoke with some of the girls that she had gotten to know at the Home. They told her that they had helped line a butterbox with satin and other decorations to be used for Faith's casket.

Violet never stopped thinking about her baby, and years later, still considered having the grave opened to see for herself if a baby was buried there. Her doctor eventually suggested that she look into it, for her own peace of mind. She was certain, though, that the Youngs would have been smart enough to put another baby's body in the butterbox. "They say that they had lots of them, so they could have done that, and my baby might just be alive." While still at the Home, Violet remembers a six-month-old baby boy named Joey. "Mrs. Young wanted me to adopt him, and through the years, I've been sorry I didn't. He had such nice grey-blue eyes. I often wondered where he went. He was born in January, or the first of February, 1940."

Because of the internal injuries sustained during the delivery of Faith

Lu Tanya, Violet was never able to bear any other children. Her husband Sterling died of a brain tumour at the age of thirty-eight, and Violet spent the next twenty-nine years nursing his mother and her own.

When asked recently about the chances of her daughter being alive, Violet said, "She probably doesn't even know she was adopted. They could hardly tell her if she was stolen, so she probably doesn't know." Over the years, she has been visited by several women searching for their birth mothers, but none was her daughter. One day, she received a telephone call that gave her a brief ray of hope. "The caller asked, 'Are you the lady on TV who is looking for your daughter?' I said, 'Yes I am…are you my daughter?' and she said, 'I think I got the wrong number.' I think she got cold feet. I've done a lot of thinking over this and I sure wonder if she is alive or not. I know she has brown eyes and dark hair because we both had those. I'm all alone now. I've got no one. My people are all dead— I've got lots of friends, but I don't have any relatives."

Over the years, Violet has hoped and believed that her daughter is alive. From the first concerns told her by Virginia that someone wanted to adopt her baby, to the unexpected death, the refusal to allow anyone to see the remains, and the "protection" of the casket until all family had left the cemetery, real doubts have lingered in Violet's mind.

There is another fact that has never been explained: the difference in the registered name of birth and death. When Faith's birth was registered, her name was recorded as Faith Lu Tanya Eisenhauer, yet on the death certificate, it reads Faith Lu Tanya Hatt—Violet's maiden name. This discrepancy was questioned several times, but no explanation was given as to why this was done, or why nothing had been done to correct it.

Although Violet never forgot her loss, she eventually accepted what had happened, and life went on—until the re-emergence of the story of the Ideal Maternity Home with the 1992 publication of the book *Butterbox Babies*. The book rekindled memories, and as more stories of the Ideal Maternity Home were exposed, Violet's hope that her baby had survived became stronger. There was now documented evidence that other mothers had been told their babies died, only to find out years later that they had been adopted, and in some cases, were reunited with their mothers when adults. "If this could happen to someone else, then why couldn't it have happened to my baby?" Violet asks. Violet told her story over and over, and it was reported in the media during the years immediately following publication of *Butterbox Babies*. With the publicity that preceded and followed the Survivors' reunion, many more people who had been connected with the Home came forward, including some who were reported to have died following birth, and have since been reunited with their birth families.

Violet gained the attention and support of many people, including Parent Finders of Nova Scotia, and Mike Slayter, then spokesperson for the group. As their friendship grew, Mike provided the support and assistance that Violet needed to once again pursue her search for the truth. The suspicious circumstances of her baby's death formed the basis of Violet's application to the Nova Scotia Department of Justice and the Department of Health to exhume the grave. Violet was visited unexpectedly by the RCMP, who told her to, "Leave everything alone, forget about it and don't bother anymore." They asked to be notified if Parent Finders or any reporters were in contact with her, and left, leaving her shocked and intimidated. "They tried to convince me that the baby is dead, to give up and not have anything to do with Parent Finders any more. Why would they do that?" Violet asks.

While still waiting for an answer almost a year later, Violet was advised that she would have to renew her application to exhume the grave, as the Department of Community Services thought that she had withdrawn her request. Finally, she received a response, but unfortunately not one that gave her much hope. The Province of Nova Scotia ultimately gave permission for the grave to be exhumed, but at her own expense, which, including subsequent DNA testing, could have amounted to close to $5,000. Medical Examiner Dr. John Butt advised the justice officials not to fund the request, as it was unlikely that an exhumation would find remains in the grave. The combination of immature bones and tissue with the area's acidic groundwater would have dissolved the child's body, so there would be nothing left to analyse. As well, Dr. Butt said he could not recommend spending public money on something that was not part of a criminal investigation. Disappointed when she received the news, Violet said, "I knew darn well they would make it so I couldn't possibly do this."

Violet was disappointed by the decision, but the adoption communities of Nova Scotia, Canada, and the United States were outraged. Letters of concern and protest began to pour in from all over North America. Although Canada was in the midst of a postal strike, letters still arrived by both fax and e-mail. In addition, the media became involved, and a local television host did a story that was televised throughout eastern Canada. Three anthropology experts indicated that there would be remains in the grave. One of them, Laird Nivon, volunteered to do the exhumation at his own expense.

The Nova Scotia Department of Justice was notified in advance when the program would be aired. That afternoon, the Deputy Minister of Justice announced that the province had reversed its decision not to fund the exhumation, based on new information, and out of compassion for Mrs. Eisenhauer. The Justice Department would accordingly assume the full costs of any DNA testing if any remains were found in the gravesite, as well as reimburse any reasonable expenses incurred by Mr. Nivon for the exhumation. At last, the way was open to bring closure to Violet's questions. If the remains (if any) in the tiny grave were not those of Faith Lu Tanya, it would mark a new beginning in the search for her.

As Violet waited in the car that cold December morning, many thoughts ran through her mind. Why were so many people willing to help her? Why were so many people interested in her story? Although not understanding, she took great comfort in knowing that she was not alone.

Violet places flowers at the monument on behalf of the birth mothers, and for her daughter, Faith Lu Tanya — August 31, 1997.

After several hours of digging, the tiny grave was discovered and the butterbox located. The cover had long since disintegrated, and one end was gone. But the two sides, the other end, and the bottom of the box, although badly deteriorated, were intact, with fragments of satin still attached to the wooden sides of the box, some discoloured, and some remarkably white. Carefully, the contents of the box were scooped out and examined. Several nails and wood fragments, and pieces of satin material were removed. The entire inside bottom of the box was covered with a layer of dirt of a different colour and texture than the dirt in the grave, which led to the suspicion that it may have been interred with the butterbox. Three fragments, plus what could have been a button or snap, and several nails, screws, and wood scraps were found, then carefully bagged and prepared to be sent to the designated DNA lab for testing. The tiny grave was then restored.

A DNA lab in Virginia was recommended by the medical examiner, and arrangements were made for the testing, which was expected to take approximately three weeks. Because of the Christmas holidays, the samples weren't sent to the lab until early January, but the results were still expected by the end of the month. It was a long wait, and then on the day that the results were expected, Violet was notified that it would now be the middle of April before anything could be done. Apparently, the lab, which was chosen because it could expedite the testing, was closing for a month, and couldn't complete the tests as expected.

Finally, on May 4, 134 days after the exhumation, the results were available. Unfortunately, after all the waiting, there was still no answer to the question of whether or not Faith Lu Tanya had indeed died, and been buried in a satin-lined butterbox. The lab reported that there was insufficient DNA in the bone fragments to successfully complete the testing and that the results were "inconclusive."

Despite this news, Violet remained undaunted. Never having believed that her daughter had died, this news served only to renew her conviction that Faith is still alive. For Violet, and many of the people who have stood beside her during this ordeal, the search for Faith Lu Tanya will go on. They believe that Faith Lu Tanya is living somewhere in North America, unaware of her origins or adoption, and unaware of the mother who continues to search and wait for her to come home.

A Second Chance

CORA

My twin sister and I were born in September 1922 to very poor parents. At birth I weighed four pounds and my sister, only two. We were indeed fortunate to have survived those early years. We were kept warm in a shoe box on the oven door of an old-fashioned wood stove, which is all there was for cooking and heat in those days. We were cared for by our mother and grandmother. Over the years, my mother had eight children.

We grew up in Barlochan, Ontario—an area of the Muskokas that doesn't even show up as a dot on the map today. We lived in houses that were provided by the farmers my father worked for (in addition to his salary).

I first went to work as a domestic when I was about fourteen years old. Those were long days, working twelve to thirteen hours—all maid work, and without any of the equipment available today. I lived in the home where I worked until I married at eighteen. Our son was born to us during the first year of our marriage.

In those days, when a girl married she did not work outside the home, and the husband made all the decisions. My husband was in the army, and was sent to Halifax. He said I was to go with him and our son was to stay with his parents, in Ontario. So that's what happened. I have regretted that decision ever since. Three years after our marriage, we separated while we were still in Halifax. I had no money to go back to Ontario. My son continued to live with my husband's parents and I was not allowed to see him at all.

I met the father of my second son, Leonard, on a bus. We had been going together for over a year when I discovered that I was pregnant. I was still legally married, as divorces to servicemen were not allowed until after the war. Since I was pregnant, I had to leave the residence where I was employed. I didn't know what to do.

I saw an advertisement for the Ideal Maternity Home in the local paper, and sent for their brochure. This seemed like the only option available at the time. There was no help of any kind, no welfare, no day nursery, no children's allowance. There was no help for a woman or girl who was alone and pregnant. Most of the families were too poor to help, even if they wanted to. The Ideal Maternity Home was a godsend for a lot of us.

The Home was a good clean place; the "ideal" place to go to have my baby. The owners, Dr. and Mrs. Young, provided the proper care for both me and my baby during and after my delivery. We never suspected that anything untoward was, or would, take place. Some of the girls, including me, had private rooms (mine was compliments of Leonard's father). Although the Home was large, there were only two or three private rooms; the rest were all dorm style.

The papers giving the power of attorney for a baby to the Youngs were signed either when you arrived or, failing that, in the case room. Half under the influence of ether, I doubt we had the understanding or even a chance to read the forms or comprehend what we were signing.

While at the Home, we were assigned chores. We were treated fairly well, considering the times. While I was at the Home, there were between forty and fifty babies there. I was assigned to work in nursery one and two—the newborn nurseries. Some of the girls were assigned to do cleaning, as well as the other work that had to be done. It seemed like the whole staff was made up of girls who had either had their baby, or were waiting to deliver. Hindsight being what it is, I think now that those little babies could have been held and played with a lot more— they were never held or played with as babies should be. Other than lying to us about our babies, the Youngs could have treated us a lot worse. Still, I don't want to give the impression that I condone what they did to us and our children.

Today, more than fifty years later, people have no concept of what it was like to live in the 1930s and 1940s, unless they went through it. I think the Youngs provided a good service until greed took over. They had five children of their own, and I feel sorry that they had to live through the scandal that surrounded the Ideal Maternity Home. Those children were also innocent victims. Their memories of their parents were probably much different than ours, not surprisingly.

While at the Home, I didn't see much of the Youngs. I know that Mrs. Young's signature is on Leonard's birth registration, but she was not at his birth. Both Dr. and Mrs. Young were in Halifax the day he was born. A lady named Stella was present, along with her assistant. Leonard was born with the cord wrapped around his neck, and he turned almost black for lack of oxygen. Stella and her assistant used basins of warm and cold water, and dipped him from one to the other. They told me that he would never survive, so when I was told two days before leaving the Home that he had died, I believed them.

Leonard's father helped pay my bill at the Ideal Maternity Home, and I saw him a few times after Leonard's birth, and death. We mourned together. Thinking of him and the possibility of marriage, we might have made it if we had had more time together after the war. I don't know if he is still living or not. When the war ended, he was shipped back home.

Since most people wanted to adopt girl babies, I could never understand why the Youngs would lie about boy babies dying, and then keep them around for years. My Leonard was one of those babies. He was born in May 1944 and was not adopted until 1946.

The years passed and those days at the Ideal Maternity Home were almost forgotten. I made a new life for myself. Little did I know that the past would resurface, and with it, bring me so much happiness.

On November 6, 1977, I received a phone call that changed my life. My son Leonard was alive! I couldn't believe the news and cried all night. I finally composed myself and phoned the number that he left, so that I could really find out if it was him. When he returned my call that afternoon, we talked for over an hour, trying to catch up on fifty-three years. Since that day, we have been in constant contact with each other by phone, fax, and e-mail.

On November 11, 1997, Leonard and his wonderful wife, Dianne, arrived at my home in Winnipeg. It was a marvellous and emotional weekend. I also learned that I have two lovely granddaughters in Florida. My eldest son and his family in Ontario adds another granddaughter, a grandson, three great granddaughters, and a great grandson.

It was another wonderful woman, Pat, Leonard's assistant, who initiated the reunion. In August 1995 while vacationing in Nova Scotia, Pat and her husband, Burt, made some inquiries about the Ideal Maternity Home. They collected information, and a copy of *Butterbox Babies*, which they gave to Leonard. He took it from there.

Given the chance to relive our lives, we would all, no doubt, do things differently. I have been given a second chance. I, and my two sons and their families, can now enjoy as much of a happy future as we are allowed.

See Leonard Glick's story, "Forward and Back to My History," on page 207.

I Can Die in Peace

MARY

It's been more than fifty-two years since I was there, and I have no bad recollections of the Ideal Maternity Home or my stay there. The atmosphere was more like being at a boarding school. I went there in July 1945, when there was an effort to operate more within the guidelines set by the province.

I was welcomed by a nurse, and assigned a room for the duration of my stay. The Home was basically run by the head nurse. She took charge of us, oversaw the running of the Home, and assigned us to various chores. I don't ever remember seeing Dr. or Mrs. Young all the time I was there.

There was no one in particular delegated to do the cooking. I'll never forget sitting at this long, bare, wooden table at lunch and looking at a pea pod and a worm floating in the broth. But we did have peaches for dessert. A short while later, an older lady and her middle-aged daughter took over the kitchen, and finally we had good meals to look forward to. The girls who could afford it paid their board, so they didn't have to work while they were at the Home. In the beginning I didn't work either, but I was bored with nothing to do. One day, I decided to mix a batch of bread. It was so well received that the head nurse gave me that as my chore. Every morning, I would mix white bread and bake it later, so we always had fresh bread. During the day, we wandered around the grounds and sometimes got permission to walk to the town of Chester. What a spectacle we must have been. We were all sizes and all ages. At night we would sit around the big room and read or play games or do puzzles. There were rarely any arguments or friction between the girls;

after all, we were all there for the same reason. There was an older handy-man working at the Home. He used to go to the store for groceries when needed, especially my yeast cakes when I forgot to order them!

Sometimes, on dreary days, I would help in the nursery on my time off. The babies were not really in A-1 condition. There wasn't much super-vision. One of the girls would take the older (three to six years or younger) children out to play in the backyard on nice days. I never saw any butterboxes. One little baby died when I was in the nursery, and we just wheeled her crib into another room. The head girl did not notify anyone at that time. Now I think how callous we were! That baby could have been mine.

We were all given aliases while we were there so no one knew for sure who was there unless we confided in each other. I was friends with one girl, right up until she passed away a couple of years ago. Some girls did fancy work—crocheting or knitting—and no one bothered them. One girl was crocheting a tablecloth; it was beautiful. The cook and her daughter and I used to talk after our work, and we would crochet and embroider. We didn't have very many rules. We really were one big "happy" family.

I don't remember much about the actual birth of my baby, except that just the nurses were there. It was an easy birth, thankfully. I used to visit my baby in the nursery and looked after her at times. Knowing about the state of care, and the shortage of people working in the nurs-ery, I hated to leave her there. (Thank God, she was adopted three months later.) I came home after ten days, and she was never mentioned again, except in my thoughts.

I am so elated to be able to say I have found my daughter after fifty-two years, thanks to my son and Bob Hartlen. I will always be indebted to them. I've kept this secret for over fifty years, and am relieved that it is finally out in the open. This makes my world complete, and I can now die in peace, knowing my life has come full circle. I feel like the father in the Bible story "The Prodigal Son," except it was my daughter who was lost and is found. I just hope we can be friends and enjoy each other while I am still alive and healthy.

See Gail's story, "Delighted to Be Found," on page 123.

Memories
of a Birth Mother

Many birth mothers who chose to go to the Ideal Maternity Home never looked back after they had their babies. They returned to their homes and families, secure in the belief that their secret was safe, and that the baby they left behind would be properly cared for and would eventually find a new home with loving parents. Very few of these young mothers had much contact with each other, as they were all given aliases while there, and were discouraged from divulging their true identities.

No one knows for sure how many expectant mothers went to the Ideal Maternity Home, but according to Hilda, who, in 1946, chose to have her baby there, many mothers came and went during her five to six month stay. Hilda recalls that the Home was nearing the end of its operation when she was there. The Youngs were in court every two to four weeks.

When Hilda discovered her pregnancy, there were very few options open to her. Almost everyone in her community knew of her pregnancy—one of her neighbours even offered to marry her. Although it would have given a name to her child, she decided that she couldn't accept, because it would just add another headache to an existing problem. Her mother was elderly at the time and had already raised ten children and two grandchildren. Hilda couldn't consider going out to work and leaving an infant for her mother to look after. She could only earn $5 or $6 a week doing housework. Her boyfriend said he would marry her if she gave the baby away. He said he couldn't take "that disgrace" home. He was just getting out of the service and gave her the money to go to the Home. He made all kinds of excuses, from the child not being his, to his parents getting a divorce and he not wanting to add to their problems. Hilda said that she couldn't take the baby to her mother either. M. Penny Spicer, a lawyer from Yarmouth, told her about the Ideal Maternity Home, where Hilda went approximately three months before her due date.

Hilda

Hilda paid a $500 fee, which was supposed to cover everything while she was there. Her boyfriend gave her $200 before he left and said he would send the rest, which he did. Before she went to the Home, he came to see her and stayed with her for a couple of days. He also went to the doctor with her and waited outside while she was examined. Hilda's doctor was really upset when he found out where she was going to have the baby, and wrote a note to Dr. Young, saying that if anything happened to Hilda, he would hold Dr. Young accountable. Hilda said, "My doctor said it was illegal. I thought he meant that it was illegal for me to go down [to the Home]. It was the Ideal Maternity Home, and all fancied up. I couldn't figure what the illegal thing was about."

Hilda couldn't remember signing anything when she arrived at the Home, except some forms wanting to know if there were any birthmarks, mental disorders, or things like that in her family. Later on, just before she was going to have the baby, she did sign papers giving the baby over to the Youngs after he was born. She also received her "new name." For her stay at the Ideal Maternity Home, she was not Hilda; she would be known as Pauline Blackburn.

Because she was able to pay for her care, it wasn't necessary for Hilda to work while at the Home, but she remembers the days being long and it was good to have something to do, so she did take a job. Besides that, if you worked, the Youngs agreed that any money earned would reduce the expenses owing. Hilda began working in the laundry on the mangling machine. It was a sit-down job, and she kept thinking that this wasn't good, that she should be getting some exercise. One day, Mrs. Young asked the girls in the laundry if one of them wanted to volunteer as the cook in the main house. Hilda volunteered. Some of the other girls worked in the nursery, some worked in the kitchen, some worked making beds, cleaning, and doing other chores. Hilda never received any money for the work, and even after her baby was gone, she had to remain at the Home, because she didn't have the money to return home.

Hilda describes how, "In the evenings when we girls were eating our meal at the table in the dining room, the Americans would come and look through a large picture window at us. They would be pointing and watching us while we sat around the table." Eventually, Ann, a girl sitting beside her said, "Don't look now, they're picking you out." "Picking us out?" Hilda said, "Picking us out for what?" Ann replied, "Well they're choosing who is going to have their baby. They pick the one who is the closest to what they look like." Hilda says, "I didn't believe it, but that was how they picked the girls...by looking through that glass window at us." She said in many cases the baby was picked long before the actual birth. Sometimes the adoptive parents stayed for a week or two, even months, for the baby to be born, then they would leave, taking the baby with them. Sometimes the babies would only be a couple of days old.

"These people who came from New York and other places wanted perfect babies. A difficult birth would be one in which nothing out of the ordinary happened in that case room," Hilda said. "I remember one girl there was jolly and happy and other times she was crying. Some of the girls would get so scared sometimes from the stories they heard from others inside the Home. I heard them too. Those stories were about the babies buried behind the Home. The only thing we could do was to say a prayer that we had a healthy baby. That didn't make me feel very good, because I also heard a story that Lila beat a young girl that came in and had a baby with a venereal disease. That baby was still there in the nursery. I saw it. They said Mrs. Young put a terrible beating on the mother. I never heard any other stories of beatings or discipline. It's hard to believe that she would do anything like that. She was so happy when a baby was born. She was also getting a lot of money for a baby. I was told by one of the girls in there that she got $2,000 for my Howard. The other big worry was what would happen if something went wrong, and would we get the chance to get out of there for help. She would never get us to Halifax in time. One night one of the girls did have a problem—she was hemorrhaging real bad. Ann and I broke up—I don't know how many—orange crates and boxes, and chopped wood down in the cellar with an axe. We worked till about two o'clock in the morning, trying to get enough hot water for them. Then we went outside and watched them pace back and forth, till finally she got all right. We really worried about that kind of thing."

According to Hilda, things were pretty good at the Home in 1946. "We had a lot of fun while we were there. We had our baths every night. There was lots of water and lots to eat. For breakfast, you could have bacon, eggs, toast, coffee, and you could have lunch any time. If you wanted, you could just lay around and talk all afternoon. My sister was allowed to come down from Halifax to visit me and see the babies. The Youngs would arrange to take us to town by bus to the show every Saturday night, if we wanted to go. Some of the girls got together and went, and we paid our own way. I only went to one show. There was always a gang of men waiting by the theatre to look at the girls and they would say terrible things and try to get the girls to go out with them. Men also used to come around the Home and try to sell lobster to the girls and take them out. After seeing that, I preferred to stay back at the Home instead of going to town to the shows. There wasn't any mail delivery to the Home, and we had to walk up the road to mail our letters at a house there. My sister used to send me money, and as long as you had your own money you could take a taxi to town. Another girl and I used to go out to town to a restaurant once in a while. She was planning to run away, which she eventually did. Her child was still at the Home, and probably would remain there because of its deformities. When I heard the stories about deformed babies not being able to stay there, I recalled those I saw in the nursery with the older children. They were three, four, and five years old, so they had been there for a long time. There weren't a lot of visitors at the Home, mainly only the inspectors and the people who wanted to adopt. The inspectors were always coming in, so we had to have our beds made up nice. They would come in and inspect our rooms, and to see if we were overworked, getting lots to eat, and if we were happy. By this time, the Youngs' home was just used for the family. In the evening, we would sit around and tell jokes, laugh and talk about everything imaginable."

Hilda remembered Lila and William's children, William, Marshall, Cyril, Isobel, and Joyce. "We used to get a real kick out of Joyce," Hilda said, laughing. "Every morning you could count on her coming in through that big sun porch at ten or ten thirty, where all of us girls were sitting, and she would look at us and say, 'You stupid things, how could you be so stupid!' It was almost like getting a peeling from your father. She was only about ten years old at the time, and was the image of her father.

Cyril and Marshall also used to come over to talk with us quite a bit. They were nice boys, but sometimes they would really get carried away and wreck the walls in the house. The Youngs had lots of money, and they didn't really seem to care. Willy would also come every once in a while. He was studying to be a lawyer. We would talk with him and tease him, asking if he was his father's lawyer yet. We got quite a charge out of the Youngs' children. They had everything. They had motorcycles, bicycles, and even their own private school right out back of the Home, and their own school teacher.

Dr. Young was a bone-setter, and if there was someone who needed his help he helped them. He didn't do too much around the Home. He didn't deliver the babies, but he did give stitches if someone needed them. He also insisted that the girls stay in bed for ten days to recover from the childbirth, although occasionally some would sneak out. I remember him as quiet; he never really gave us a smile or a 'How do you do?' He kept the books in the office. He also did most of the ordering, the groceries and things like that, as well as the hiring. He also did a lot of fishing on his yacht, and would often take people out fishing. One day, he came home after a fishing trip, and I thought I was in the middle of the Atlantic Ocean. There were so many flounders everywhere. They were boiling them on the stove and feeding them to the hens that they kept to supply the Home with eggs.

"Mrs. Young was very pleasant when she came around in the morning, and when a baby was born, she was really happy. In the evening, sometimes she would go to the piano and play and sing songs. She was kind of comical in some ways. They were Seventh Day Adventists, and they never drank coffee, only lime juice. But they never tried to force their beliefs on us. The home had a big hall and a big sun porch, and the most modern equipment and fancy machinery—all gifts of appreciation—and Mrs. Young didn't know how to use any of it. She would get really mad if you crossed her. Some of the girls ran away after they had their babies, and never paid. When that happened, she would call in the Mounties and was usually very upset. She ran a tight ship."

Like most of the women who stayed at the Home, Hilda got to know many of the people who worked there. One of the older workmen befriended her during her stay. She remembered him as Bumstead, and referred to him as a nice older man who worked as a janitor. He had a little place of his own on the property and had a dog and some cats. When she was working at the Youngs' home, he would sometimes come over to see her. The night her son was born, he brought Hilda a package of cigarettes. She remembered telling him, "He is only five and a half pounds," to which he laughed and said, "Bad weeds grow fast."

"They didn't hire a lot of people to work at the Home, but Mrs. Young did have real graduate nurses—Jenny, Mrs. LeBlanc, Mrs. Keating, and Elizabeth Gillis. Mrs. Gillis was the nurse who worked out of the front office when you entered the Home, and she took your name, and put your money in the safe. Mrs. Young was there with most of the girls when they had their babies, but Jenny did most of the helping for the ones that I can remember. Jenny and Mrs. Keating both had their children there and both continued to work at the Home. Both had daughters who were five or six years old by then, and went to school in Chester."

The night that Hilda had her baby, June 3, 1946, she remembers an American woman being with her while she delivered her baby. The woman held Hilda's hand the whole time, and Mrs. Young was called in for the delivery. "That was two o'clock in the morning, but by the time she arrived, she was too late—Howard, my son, was already born." The American woman, who was sitting beside Hilda's bed, said to Mrs. Young,

"I want this baby. I was here when he was born, I've been with her through the whole delivery." Mrs. Young replied that she couldn't have the baby, that he was already spoken for. Hilda realized then that what Ann had told her was true, they did pick you out through those glass windows. In the morning, while lying upstairs in bed, Hilda said that she could hear the American ladies saying things like, "My baby is going to be born tomorrow. He's going to be here tomorrow." She adds, "You know, they sounded right happy about it too, almost like they were going to have the baby themselves."

Hilda recalls, "We weren't allowed to see our babies after they were born. I did, however, see Howard twice. Jenny brought him into me and let me have him for about five minutes. If I had held him any longer, I never would have been able to let him go. I called out to Jenny to come and get him. Three days later, I saw him again, being wheeled past my room. Just before that, I had sneaked down to the nursery and there was a man there and he was holding my baby. As I was peeking around the door, he saw me and asked me, 'Are you worrying about your baby?' I said, 'Yes.' I knew his name was Newman, the man who was supposed to be adopting my child. I saw the name on the papers. He said, 'Don't worry about your baby. I will take good care of him.' He was giving him his bottle, and that was the last time I saw him. They went back into the nursery and I went back to my room. I never saw him again and never knew when he was taken away. I still have the paper here from when he entered the United States.

Howard (4 years old—1950).

"When Howard was born, he was one of about 135 babies in the main nursery at the time. This nursery was the one where most of the newborns were kept. There was another smaller one for the older babies. There would have been maybe ten there at that time. These weren't really babies, some were probably four or five years old. There were a couple that probably would never have been adopted. Their hands and feet were crippled. They were still there when I left the Home. I remember one evening in this nursery, they had stew for supper. There was a young girl there, about fourteen or fifteen years old, who was feeding the children. She had a spoon and a big pot and was going around feeding them from the spoon. When I asked her what she was doing, she said that Mrs. Young told her to feed them. I told her to get bowls and spoons for each of them, that they could feed themselves, but she just said that Mrs. Young would be mad.

"Most of the babies there seemed to be healthy, but spent most of the time in their cribs. I never saw them outside except when Jenny took them out to take their pictures, never just for the fresh air. There wasn't a lot of play time for the babies there either.

"After Howard was gone, I also helped out in the nursery. I looked after about twenty-five babies. There used to be more girls working there, but with the Home getting ready to close, some of them left, so there really wasn't anyone there to take care of these babies. Dr. Young got after me once for using too much Johnson's baby powder and Vaseline; he said I was going to bankrupt him. I didn't pay any attention to him— those babies needed to be kept clean.

"My brother had been overseas in the service, and had just come back home. When he asked where I was, my mother said I was in a home in Chester, and didn't have the money to come home. He sent me $100 and I finally got out of there. If it wasn't for him, I probably would have had to hitchhike, because I don't think Dr. Young would have helped me.

"When I finally got home, I saw some stories in the Halifax paper about babies being found floating in Halifax Harbour. Whether they had been thrown overboard or not I didn't know, all I could think was that maybe Howard was one of them. Some people speculated that the babies had come from the Home. This would have been near the end of 1946. I kept wondering if they [the adoptive parents] were afraid they were going to get caught with the babies and threw them overboard. It left an empty feeling in me for quite awhile, not knowing whether or not he was really adopted or even if he was alive. It was terrible not

Hilda and son Howard visit the site
of the former Ideal Maternity Home "together"—July 21, 1997.

knowing what had happened to him."

It was another four years before Hilda would have the answer to that question and finally stop worrying. One day, she got a call to go to Yarmouth, to sign Howard's adoption papers. Her brother took her there by boat and they went to the court house. The lawyer, M. Penny Spicer, the same lawyer who told her about the Ideal Maternity Home four years earlier, told her that she could still get her baby back—and her $500—if she wanted. Hilda felt that after four years, Howard's adoptive family were the ones who cared for him and loved him; she felt she couldn't take him away from them now. She also thought that if there was any money to be had, Howard's family deserved it. At least she finally knew that he was safe, and that he did make it to the United States and wasn't one of those babies found in the harbour. But she never stopped thinking about him, what he was doing, how he was, and where he was.

Hilda never had any other children, but throughout the years she cared for her sister's children. She would have all of them together, tending to them, washing them, getting them ready for bed. They still came to her house even when they were bigger. Hilda eventually married in 1949, and told her husband about Howard. Her husband already had two grown sons, almost her age. He had offered to take Howard at the age of four, when she got the call from the lawyer. He told her to bring the child home, but she thought, to what? They weren't married, he wasn't Howard's father, and he was a heavy drinker. His own boys fought with him.

When she returned home after her stay at the Ideal Maternity Home, Hilda remained on Cape Forchu for years. She always believed that some day Howard would come knocking at the door, looking for his mother. She believed it so strongly, that she would often get dressed up, just in case, so she would be at her best when he finally arrived. For her it was making believe, but also knowing in her heart that her dream would come true. It was those dreams that kept her going at times, until that day finally came, when he did arrive on her doorstep, and back into her life.

See Howard Cooper's story, "A Reason to Come Home," on page 196.

Two Mothers Reflect

adeline and Barbara lived apart for fifty-one years, never knowing where the other was, or even if their paths would ever cross again. Their story started in 1942, when Madeline made the decision to go to the Ideal Maternity Home to give birth to her child.

Madeline was only twenty-two years old when she went to the Home, following a wartime romance with a young Scottish sailor. She remembers that on the winter night that she gave birth, part of the roof of the Home had been torn away to permit renovations. Madeline also recalls that a young girl who worked at the Home brought Madeline's baby girl to her secretly one night while the Youngs were away. (After their births, the babies were kept in the nursery, and their mothers were not allowed to see them or have any contact with them, although many, like Madeline, managed to break that rule.) Madeline remembers sitting behind the piles of laundry, rocking her baby and crying, wishing that she could keep her, but knowing that it was impossible.

When Madeline left the Ideal Maternity Home, she returned to work as a maid for a couple in Halifax. She later married an electrician and moved to Montreal and then Windsor, which was only a few miles from where her daughter Barbara was raised.

Over the years, not a day passed that Madeline did not think about the baby girl that she gave birth to, and rocked in her arms for a brief time. Little did she know then, that fifty-one years after giving birth, she would be sitting with her daughter beside her again.

Barbara at 4 years old,
building sand castles and cupcakes.

Barbara (5 years old) always enjoyed spending quality time
with her adoptive father, who passed away just five years after
this photo was taken.

Barbara and her birth mother
(Madeline) reunited in person on
Mother's Day, 1993,
after finding each other
only three months earlier.

Barbara at first meeting with birth
mother and her four birth brothers
on Mother's Day.

Despite the good reputation of the Ideal Maternity Home, Madeline had heard stories and rumours about babies being buried nearby, but, like others, she believed they were the unfortunate babies that died in childbirth. It was decades later, after reading the book *Butterbox Babies*, that she first read stories of abuse, neglect, and of mysterious deaths surrounding unhealthy babies who were deemed unfit for adoption or sale.

The story of Madeline's stay at the Ideal Maternity Home is a sad one, but something was rectified on Mother's Day, 1993, when Madeline finally met the baby girl she bore fifty-one years before. At age seventy-three, it was like a miracle to be in her daughter's home in Ontario, smiling at the daughter she feared she had lost forever. For Barbara, it was equally exciting to be there, hugging the mother she had never known. During that first meeting, the two women, both grandmothers, exchanged a lifetime of stories and experiences and became part of each other's lives again.

Although many babies born at the Ideal Maternity Home were adopted and taken across Canada and into the United States, Barbara was adopted by a couple in Halifax and remained in Nova Scotia. Barbara's adoptive father died when she was ten years old and her adoptive mother never remarried. Barbara married a mechanic and part-time stock-car racer and together they raised three children. It was in the Halifax newspaper that Barbara read a "Birthday Wish" for a long-lost daughter—giving her date of birth—which was placed there by Madeline and her family. Barbara recognized that the wish was for her and responded to it. The rest is history. Both Madeline and Barbara believe that they are fortunate that they survived the Ideal Maternity Home, and that they have found each other again.

Although they live in different provinces, Madeline and Barbara continue to be part of each other's lives. In August 1997, both attended the Survivors Reunion in Chester, Nova Scotia, and saw part of their story portrayed in the play *Aftermath*.

D O R I S

*D*oris remembers the tragedy that struck her and her
husband in 1945, which resulted in her becoming an adoptive mother: "On April 23, 1945, when our third baby was
born and lived for only ten hours, my husband and I were extremely
unhappy. I couldn't bring myself to even look at any one else's baby.
The truth of the matter is that I was jealous. We felt even worse when
our friends brought their new baby home from hospital.

"While I was in the hospital, someone mentioned adopting a baby at
the Ideal Maternity Home in East Chester. They told me that all you
had to do was to go there and pick out a baby, and you could bring it
home the same day. At first the idea didn't appeal to us, but as time
went on, we talked about it a little bit more, and the more we talked,
the more it seemed like a good idea. One thing led to another, and on
June 22, 1945, my husband and I borrowed my father's car, collected
together some baby clothes, and headed to East Chester.

"My husband knew where the Home was as he had driven past it many
times when he was trucking lumber to Halifax. When we arrived at the
Home, we were greeted by a very friendly lady, who turned out to be Lila
Young. She listened to our story of losing our baby and how we desperately
wanted another child. She was very understanding and took us into a large
room with cribs and baskets lined all around the room. There were about
forty babies, of all ages, ranging from about two or three months up to
about twelve months old. We were elated, but as we looked them over, none
of them seemed right for us, especially the older ones. They were just lying
flat on their backs, and weren't nearly as active as we thought they should
have been. We spent a long time looking the babies over. It felt like we were
in a grocery store looking for just the right box of cereal. All of a sudden a
nurse came into the room carrying a tiny bundle in her arms. That tiny
bundle was a baby boy who was just nine days old and seemed to be very

hungry. He was chewing on his fists. From that first moment that we saw him, as far as we were concerned, he was the winner. We picked up this little bundle, and claimed him for our son. They dressed him in the clothes we brought with us, and we filled out and signed the necessary papers right there. We lost our hearts to many there, but this skinny little baby would not let go, so we took him home in a butterbox. He was so starved, his fingernails were purple. It was just like we had been told—you really could take your baby home the same day. Throughout the whole procedure, Mrs. Young was very attentive and pleasant.

Robert at 3 months old.

"Our baby was the most starved child that I had ever seen. We fed him Pablum mixed with his milk formula and eventually we got him and his hungry little tummy satisfied. In later years, after hearing the stories about some of the babies at the Home, we figured that he must have been one of those babies who was living on molasses and water, and probably headed for a butterbox, like others supposedly did before him.

"He had been born at the Grace Maternity Hospital in Halifax, and then taken to the Ideal Maternity Home when he was two days old. His mother had not signed any papers for him to be adopted, but Mrs. Young assured us that we would be safe in taking him home. Our little boy had no name, so we had to find a name for him. I wanted to name him Harry, after my mother's brother who died early in life, so we tried all ways to get

Robert at 15 years old.

a name that would go with Harry. As much as we tried, we couldn't find one, so in the end we named him Robert Melbourne. Once he had a name, we filled out the papers and got his birth certificate registered.

"After we had Robert for about three months (and he wasn't hungry anymore), a lady from the Children's Aid came one day to see how we were getting along with our new baby. I guess it was really to investigate us as new parents. She brought with her the papers that his mother had signed. She told us that after she had sent him to the Ideal Maternity Home, his mother tried to get him back, but there was nothing that could be done and no one at the Home would help her. Eventually, she signed the release papers. She had given Robert a name—Harry Edward McLaughlin. It was ironic that she had given him the name Harry, the same name that we had wanted to give him. By this time, we had already registered his name as Robert Melbourne Hirtle, and it was too late to change it.

Robert (1997).

"We were not wealthy by any means, but our riches were having this beautiful baby and our loving home. By the way, this little fellow was apparently not saleable, because we didn't pay anyone for him. It didn't cost us a cent when we got Robert from the Ideal Maternity Home. I guess they were glad that we came along when we did and wanted to take him. Dr. Young wasn't there the day we went to Chester so we did all of our dealings with Lila Young. We didn't even have to pay the lawyer who represented us at the court hearing for the adoption, which took place about a year after we brought Robert home. We have always thanked God that we decided to go to the Ideal Maternity Home and get Robert. We had made the right decision and maybe even saved this baby's life.

Today, he is a husky, six-foot-tall man. He has always been our son and I know he appreciates what we did for him. Before my husband died, he mentioned that we probably saved our son's life in June 1945.

THE DAUGHTERS SPEAK

I Was Not Adoptable!

B R E N D A

On May 18, 1915, a teenage Scottish lass (who had come to Canada with her older sister), married a Canadian soldier. Catherine and Willard Walton settled in Dartmouth, Nova Scotia, where Willard worked at the shipyards after the end of World War I. After some twenty-six years of marriage without children, they decided to look into adoption. This was not an easy decision at their age (she was forty-five and he was fifty-six), but eventually they decided to adopt a baby from the Ideal Maternity Home in Chester, Nova Scotia. When they visited the Home, they were shown a number of babies in the nursery, among them twin boys. When Catherine and Willard expressed an interest in the twins, they were told that the boys were not adoptable as they were ill. Willard was drawn to another baby, who looked up at him from her crib, smiled, and reached up her arms. He reached down, picked up the baby, and announced, "We'll take this one." That was truly my lucky day, and the beginning of a happy and loving family life. Being "instant" parents, the Waltons had to buy the necessary items for a baby on the way home.

Soon after, I became very ill and had a bad rash over my entire body. The scabs on my head were so bad that my hair had to be shaved off. The doctor put me in hospital to find out what was wrong. I was tied to the crib so I wouldn't scratch, and still bear the scars on my right wrist where the ties were attached. After several days in the hospital, I was dying. My dad came to the hospital and, against the doctor's wishes, insisted on taking me home. On the way, he stopped by a local pharmacy and described my condition to the pharmacist, who suggested they feed me a certain powdered milk, as his own child had had a similar illness that had been helped by the milk. Dad bought the milk and made me a bottle. After I downed the second bottle of milk, because I was so hungry, my mom became afraid that it would kill me. "At least she will die with a full stomach," dad said. The milk worked and my eczema cleared up. Because I was ill, the Youngs offered to take me back, but my parents wouldn't hear of it. In September 1941, my adoption was finalized.

When I was about three, we moved to a small community in Port Elgin, New Brunswick, where dad cleared land and built our home. From the time I started to walk I had a limp, and although the doctor couldn't find anything wrong, the pain would get severe if I tried to do anything physical, such as sports.

My parents told me about being adopted before I started school, but it really didn't sink in. They said I was special because they had chosen me. Later on I was told by some kids at school that I was different. My mom said I was different because I was adopted—they couldn't have a baby of their own, so they chose one that was born to someone who was unable to take care of me. This was alright with me, and I didn't think anymore about it.

I sang at a very young age and this continued through my teens and adult life. I enjoyed singing and sang in the church, at school, and even on the radio with "Don Messer and the Islanders," from the time I was nine. My dad frequently worked out of town as a carpenter on large jobs, so my mom and I spent a lot of time together. My parents were always supportive of me in whatever I did. When I was fourteen, I won first prize in the local music festival, and a scholarship to Mount Allison University in Sackville, New Brunswick. I did this three years in a row, and, after I graduated from high school, I worked as secretary to the librarian in the university library, so that I could continue my singing lessons.

I was still having a lot of pain in my knees and hips, and finally a doctor realized that I had a physical problem. I had been born with both hips dislocated, and one leg shorter than the other, which was the cause of the pain and the limp. I had surgery on one hip when I was

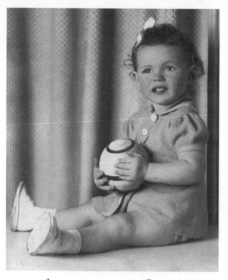

Brenda (1 year old) — Dec 1941.

Brenda (6 years old), with adoptive
mother — 1946.

Brenda
(17 years old)
—1957.

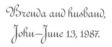

Brenda and husband,
John — June 13, 1987.

Brenda and John's three sons:
Hudson, Scott, and Shawn.

fifteen, but it was unsuccessful. By the time I was eighteen, I had arthritis in both hips. At this time, my dad, who was then in his seventies, walked to work at the local sawmill every day to put me through school. In February 1960, my dad suffered a heart attack. He recovered, but while in hospital they found he had cancer and gave him three months to live. I was devastated. My mom had been sick all her adult life with angina and dad had worked hard to pay medical bills, etc. He had always looked after both of us.

I loved doing things with my dad, like getting wood for winter, which we hauled from the woods with a horse, then split and piled. Just to know my dad was not going to be with us was the hardest thing I have ever had to face. He passed away in August that same year. I will always remember standing at his grave holding the Union Jack as they played the Last Post. I was nineteen years old and had lost the most important person in my life.

Soon after, my mom and I sold our home and moved to Sackville. We lived together in an apartment until I moved to Halifax to work. I met my first husband there, and went to BC in May 1961 to be married. My mom passed away two weeks after I got married. Seven years and two young sons later, the marriage ended in divorce. In 1969, I met and married my present husband, John. We have a son, Shawn, who is almost twenty-four years old. When he was a year old, I had my right hip replaced, and in 1983 the left hip was done. Both hips were replaced again in 1990.

I had never really thought about searching for my birth family, until my sister-in-law sent me a copy of an item from a Vancouver paper about a lady who found her birth mother with the help of Parent Finders. I wrote to them on March 12, 1997. After several conversations, they told me they had a information on a woman who might be my birth mother. My birth certificate showed that I was delivered by Lila Young. I remembered a news story that I had heard about a Lila Young and her home for unwed mothers in East Chester. The story told of how they had found butterboxes in the yard of the Home with babies' bodies in them. I immediately looked through the papers I had from my adopted parents.

I thought of my birth mother more and more as the years went by, and wondered how her life had been, and if I had any half-brothers or sisters. There was no way I wanted to disrupt her life, but I wondered if she thought about me and what my life had been like.

I was certainly fortunate to have been brought up by such a loving and caring family. I have wondered about my heritage and what I can pass on to my children. I was certainly one of the lucky ones coming out of the Ideal Maternity Home; it could have been me in one of those boxes. My parents told me that I had spent the first nine months of my life in a crib.

After being given possible names by Parent Finders, I spent hours at our local library looking in telephone books in an effort to find my birth mother. Finally, a woman living in Toronto matched some of the information on my adoption papers. There was a good chance that she was my mother, so I made notes on what to say to her and resolved to try to be sensitive to how she would respond. Would there be denial or acceptance? She and her husband, who had died recently, had three children—two boys and a girl. Had she told the children about me? So many questions and only one way to get the answer.

I decided that I would call at 6.45 A.M. on Wednesday, April 16; that would make it 9:45 A.M. in Toronto. I asked the person who answered the phone her name, and told her that my name was Brenda and I was calling on a personal matter. I told her I was researching my family history, and that I had been adopted and brought up as an only child. I said I had reason to believe that she could be my birth mother. She replied, "Well, I had a baby girl I had to give up a lot of years ago." I told her my birth name, date of birth, and where I had been born. She said that I was her daughter. We talked for almost an hour and she told me about her family, and I about mine. She said she would love to meet me sometime and to at least write to her. She took my phone number as well. She had told her husband about me (he was not my birth father) and that it didn't matter to him, but she never told her children. She said my birth father had worked at a local theatre, and when she told him she was pregnant, he told her he was married. She sounded so warm and loving and said I had made her day. She had often thought of me and hoped I had had a good life. She is now seventy-eight years old. I thanked God for finding her and that she was happy I did.

After our conversation on April 16, I wrote to my birth mother and sent a couple of recent photographs. A week and a half later I received a letter postmarked Toronto. It was in a small envelope and wasn't very thick, so I knew before I opened it that it could be disappointing. She had written on a small piece of white paper, "Received your letter. Sorry to inform you that I have no interest in setting up a relationship with you at this time in my life. Sorry to disappoint you, but this is the way I feel. Please do not attempt to contact me further." I can only assume that she had confided in someone and they advised her not to continue our relationship. It certainly didn't sound like the woman I spoke with on the phone. At the moment, I don't know if I should acknowledge her letter or not.

John and I have worked hard to raise our sons and make a home for them. I see the values that we have instilled in them through our lives together. I know that if my adoptive parents were looking down on us they would be proud.

Bittersweet Reunion

My name is Betty and yes, I am a Survivor of the Ideal Maternity Home. I was born on March 20, 1941. I was six months old when my parents came to the Home, chose me, and took me home with them to Dartmouth, Nova Scotia. I always knew that I was adopted and most of the time it never really bothered me, except when I was extremely unhappy, or when someone called me a "bastard." When that happened, I wanted my real mom. My dad was a wonderful person. He was a Merchant Marine, so we didn't see him very much, but it was always a joyful time when we did. He loved me dearly, and I'll always be grateful to him. He died when he was sixty-nine years old. My mother had one son of her own, who was five years older than me. She adopted me when I was six months old, then adopted another daughter three years younger than me, and a boy who is seventeen years younger. She would take in anyone who was in need. I never understood this, as she wasn't an "ideal" parent and we often had to do for ourselves. Even though I give her credit for taking us, I have never understood her intentions. There are things in my childhood that are too painful to think about.

Despite everything that happened during those years, I thank my mother from the bottom of my heart for taking me from the Home, as I am almost sure that otherwise I would not be alive today. At six months, I weighed only ten pounds and had rickets. My mother says she worked very hard so that I would walk one day, and I did. She certainly had love in her heart for me at that time.

When I was fifteen we moved to Montreal. When I was older I made inquiries about my birth parents during visits to Nova Scotia, but was always met with silence when I mentioned the maternity home. I wrote to the provincial Department of Community Services for information about my natural parents about fourteen years ago, but was given little information. I was very disappointed, but even after searching for my birth mother without luck for the last thirty years, I had never given up.

I am now married and the mother of three children of my own and still live just outside of Montreal. In 1996, after applying to have the name on my Nova Scotia birth certificate officially changed to that of my adoptive parents, I was told there was no record that I had been legally adopted. They couldn't find any papers. After hearing about changes in Nova Scotia's Adoption Act from a relative, I wrote to Community Services for more information. I had written to them in 1983 but was told only that my mother was from Digby County and that all the records had been destroyed in a fire years ago. Surely they must have known that I had not been legally adopted from their own records. They, however, did not choose to share that with me.

Betty (approx. 4 years old).

In January 1997, I received a letter from Community Services indicating that I had not been legally adopted and was given more information about my birth mother—information that I should have been entitled to years ago. They also gave me the address of Parent Finders Nova Scotia. I immediately sent Parent Finders a letter containing the information that I had just received from Community Services.

Mike Slayter, spokesperson for Parent Finders Nova Scotia, phoned me on February 5 to acknowledge receipt of my letter and told me that

Parent Finders would help me with my search and that their motto was "We never give up." Mike also told me of a colleague of his he claimed to be the best researcher in Canada. Her name was Faith. The next day, Faith telephoned to say she was sure that she had found my birth mother. There are no words that could describe that moment. Feelings suddenly

surfaced that I never knew existed; tremendously good feelings. I was on cloud nine. Faith gave me all the information she had, including a phone number for the woman they were sure was my birth mother.

At first, my birth mother denied ever having any children, and I was so disappointed. But, with the help of Mike, who, with extraordinary sensitivity and understanding was able to talk to her after I had called, everything turned out wonderfully. I phoned my birth mother again, and we were both relieved. We agreed to call and write to each other. I wanted very much to meet her, yet realized that she needed time to adjust. We arranged to meet on February 25. On February 24, my husband, Claude, who supported and encouraged me through all of this, drove me from Montreal to Halifax. I met my birth mother on February 25 and spent four marvellous hours with her. I simply cannot describe in words how I felt. After so many years of waiting and hoping, my dream had finally come true. My birth mother is not in good health, and she felt that she wasn't able to share our story with her own family, so it stayed confidential. She was, unfortunately, encumbered with guilt, like so many others. I felt that I must respect her wishes, but deep down I would love to have her near me and make up for lost time. She's a fantastic person. We agreed to keep in touch, and I only wish I had been able to find her ten years ago, when she was healthier.

Betty—14 years old.

Even with the fulfillment of dreams, however, there is always the outside chance that the dreams will fade or the bubble will burst. Unfortunately, things happened that didn't allow for the confidentiality I had promised. Because of that, following the joy of reunion, I was subjected to the pain of being disowned in April. I thought I was prepared for anything, but we are never ready for another rejection. In June, I received another call from my birth mother, telling me that her family was now aware of me, there was no more need for secrecy, and I could come back. In August, I returned to Nova Scotia and met with a fantastic family, but my mother is still very distant with me.

When I asked about my father, she said, "What you don't know won't hurt you; leave things as they are." But I feel it's my right to know. I am not complaining, as she did open the door, and I now have my roots and an extremely loving family, thanks to her.

What hurts me the most is her refusal to let her friends know about me. Why should her friends be more important than her own flesh and blood? I guess it's the little girl inside of me who refuses to understand.

I realized after a long time that in an instant I had changed my mother's life forever. I am sure she had buried the past deeply inside, confident that she could end her cozy life in peace. I came along and exposed her hiding place—the pride, the guilt, the shame. I am the living secret that she wanted to remain hidden. With all the risks, it is important for others not to give up their search for their birth parents, but they must be careful. We can hurt ourselves and others without realizing it, but in the long run, it's all worth it.

Betty and Claude
at the Survivors' Reunion, July 1998.

Lonely but Loved

KATHLEEN LORRAINE BOUTILIER

ot all of the babies adopted from the Home were happy throughout all of their lives. Although some had loving parents, they were still lonely; closeness and family contact was lacking. For others, there was a terrible longing to find that special person who would reach out and make everything all right for them.

I was born Patricia Ann Carr on Wednesday, June 16, 1943, at the Ideal Maternity Home in East Chester, Nova Scotia. I was there for almost eleven months until, on May 9, 1944, Annie Boutilier of Marriott's Cove came to the Home looking for a baby, and took me home with her to live on the family farm. Annie was in her late 40s, a reluctant empty-nester looking for company now that her children had grown up. Although the Ideal Maternity Home provided her with that, she sometimes wondered about the conditions there. She used to say that there wasn't enough help to look after the children, just one nurse for something like twenty-two babies.

On September 29, 1945, Annie and Reuben Boutilier legally adopted me, and changed my name to Kathleen Lorraine Boutilier. Mother told me that she picked me out of the gaggle of babies in the Home's nursery, almost like picking a puppy out of a pet store window. She said that I was the cutest baby there, and that's why she picked me. Although my parents checked out all the babies to see if anything was wrong with them before making their final choice, shortly after the adoption they found out that I had both a hearing impairment and a speech problem. Unfortunately, they didn't have a lot of money, and were not able to do anything about my condition. It wasn't until 1972 that I was finally able to get hearing aids, which I now wear in both ears.

Kathleen—14 months old.

Annie and Reuben had four children of their own; three boys and one girl. I grew up thinking that their daughter Beatrice was my real mother. For as long as I can remember, she had the last word, telling me what to do and how to do it, but we still got along pretty well. Dad worked in Mahone Bay at the shipyards until he retired when I was about two or three years old. My dad was born in 1877, and was an old man by then. Mother was eighteen years younger than dad and was a hard-working housewife, bringing up her five children and managing our home.

Marriott's Cove is a pretty setting, and I remember even as a young child the sunsets, the moon shining on the water at night, and piles of snow in the winter. We lived on a large farm with big gardens that provided much of our food. We had a couple of horses, two cows, three pigs, hens and chickens, a dog, and about thirty cats. These were both house cats and barn cats—they were everywhere, and we loved them.

Because of my speech problems, I didn't start school until 1951, when I was eight years old. Growing up, I spent most of my time alone; there were no other children to play with. The rest of Annie and Reuben's children were all older than I was. James and Aubrey had gone off to war, Beatrice had gone to Montreal to work, and Wesley was working in Chester. Dad and mother always got along well. He and mother used to come out to the playhouse (that dad had made me when I was small) on Sunday afternoons to keep me company, as there weren't any other kids my age around the cove.

Dad and I were very close, and we spent a lot of time together. We would go out in the boat and row around the cove, feed the animals together, and I would even help him make hay. We used to go for hay-wagon rides in the summer, and in winter we always had sleigh rides. Dad and mother also used to take me for train rides to Mahone Bay, where we shopped at Bill's Store and would then continue on to Tantallion to visit my Uncle Murray. Dad and I used to walk to the little store in the community for candy and treats, and at one time, when we had a truck, we went from house to house selling things. Once we had two boys staying with us and mother bought some bananas. One of the boys ate all of his banana and then wanted half of mine. I decided to put the banana on the chopping block and he tried to cut it with the double-headed axe. Unfortunately, he almost cut off my thumb. Mother was there and wrapped my hand in her apron and rushed me off to the doctor in Chester. Dad and mother were always there when I needed them.

Kathleen—8 years old.

Dad was diagnosed with cancer in 1955. I used to sit with him for hours. As time passed, he continued to weaken and by that November, the only nourishment he could take was what we could feed him with a spoon. Finally, on January 30, 1956, with mother and me sitting beside him, he passed away. I really missed my dad.

The older children looked after the farm as mother couldn't afford to run it alone. By that time the animals had been sold, and with only a small pension, mother really couldn't manage the farm anymore and had to go to work. Shortly after, she got sick and went back to the farm to live until it was eventually sold. After the farm was gone she moved to Chester to a smaller house. She was diagnosed with cancer in 1954 and on April 26, 1981, she passed away. My mother was always good to me and I miss both her and dad very much.

Kathleen—12 years old.

Kathleen at Reunion reception,
August 29, 1997.

I was about ten or eleven years old when our minister told me I was adopted, and my mother admitted it was true. I was very upset.

As a young girl, I used to visit the Youngs' home with my mother. Lila always treated me well, as did Dr. Young. Lila always called me her little girl. I remember mother saying that during the eleven months I was at the Home, I lay in my crib a lot in wet diapers, which made my skin rough and dry.

I was married in February 1960, and over the next ten years I had five children: Vincent, Gwendolyn, Michael, Kayangela, and Jaunita. It wasn't easy bringing up a family of this size with very little money and a husband who was hard on all of us. In May 1972, I left him and we were divorced. In 1975, I remarried, this time to a very nice man. We did everything together. I guess that I wasn't meant to enjoy this happiness, as he was killed in a car accident in 1982.

Left alone, I went to work as a cashier, but due to my failing health I stopped working in 1994. Now I fill my days doing crafts, and knitting and crocheting for my children.

I wasn't aware of the Butterbox Babies story until the fall of 1988, when I saw my picture in the paper in a publicity photo that was taken at the Ideal Maternity Home in the early 1940s. I was shocked to see the picture and to read the story. I contacted Bette Cahill, the author of the book *Butterbox Babies*, and then reporters came out to my home in Sackville to interview me. From that time the story has continued; I have met more people who were connected with the Home, heard their stories and experiences, and been part of the ongoing quest to find out the truth.

I don't know who my birth parents are. I continue to search, and continue to hope that one day I will find some of my birth family and have the chance to share in their lives and they in mine.

Because of You

J A N I C E   L Y N N   S T R E E T

J think my adoptive parents might have been unique in that they not only adopted me, but also two others from the place ironically called the "Ideal" Maternity Home. Thanks to them I grew up with a big sister, Donna, and a younger brother, Dick. We were a family in the truest sense and always will be.

Mom was intelligent, hardworking, talented, and full of love for us. She had a sense of humour, and style, and instilled the same in us, along with a high sense of values. She spent endless hours making beautiful clothes for us, led the junior choir in which we sang at the Chester Baptist Church from 1946 to 1949, and also made the choir gowns, which were still being used after her death in 1983. We not only received her warmth and capacity to show love, but also received the same from her whole family and grew up with a total sense of belonging. We were her children! I truly believe that if she had known everything that went on at the maternity home it would have broken her heart. I believe she did not know.

Dad was very proud of us, and when Dick died in a highway accident in 1969, he was heartbroken. Later, he was recognized by the government of Nova Scotia for his efforts against drunk drivers. He worked hard to provide for us and loved to show us off. I will never know why he showed me my Release for Adoption papers when I was seventeen, but he did. With that knowledge, along with information dropped now and then by mom, I was able, years later, to track down my birth parentage. Even so, when I found my birth mother, I made the choice not to tell mom. I never wanted her to doubt my love for her; never wanted her to wonder whose daughter I was—who my real mother was. She was my "real mother" and always will be. She was the right mother for me. I am as much like her as any birth child could be.

Our parents always told us we were special because they picked us out from all of the other babies. They first went to the Home to pick out a boy, but instead chose Donna. The second time they went to pick out a boy, I was standing in a crib with my arms out to them and they took me home. The third time we all went and came home with Dick. I wonder—who did the real choosing?

I had known my birth mother's name (Lila), my birth name, and the name of my birth mother's brother, who had witnessed my Release for Adoption document. I never saw that document again. It was not among the various papers that were given to us by our mother in August 1980, when I knew the time had come to begin my search.

When Donna and I asked mom for our files, she gave them to us— no questions asked. It was mom who had told me earlier that the witness was my birth mother's brother (my birth uncle), and she also revealed that my birth mother had married about a year after I was born. Without these two pieces of information, I doubt that my search would have been successful.

Acting on a hunch while in Halifax three days later, I obtained my birth mother's married name by making random phone calls to people with the same last name as my birth uncle (which was the same as my birth name). When a woman who sounded about my age answered my third call, I asked her if her husband had an aunt named Lila. He did! She gave me her married name and left the phone to find the address. I was amazed that it had been so easy. My amazement turned to panic as I heard her voice again, asking me why I wanted it. Without even thinking I heard myself say, "Because she is an old friend of my mother's and they have lost touch." My guardian angel must have been at work. I got the address. My birth mother was living in the same town as she had been when I was born!

Armed with this information, my sister-in-law and I went to the registrar general's office on an impossible mission—getting our original birth certificates. We failed, of course, but while the clerk was searching she left an open ledger on the counter and we saw Donna's birth name in it. I remember feeling that somehow that made her more real. I did receive a marriage license number for my birth mother. I had the right person, although a few minutes later at Social Services I was discouraged from thinking so. They also denied any knowledge of wrongdoing at the Home even though I had known about the article in the *Montreal Standard*, but not its contents, for many years.

They did offer to put my name in the adoption registry, and three weeks later, after I had returned to Calgary, they wrote to say there was no evidence that I had ever been at the Home. They did not know that our family had spent numerous Sunday afternoons visiting the Youngs while we were growing up. But we were totally unprepared for the revelations in the book *Butterbox Babies* when it was published.

Leaving Social Services, we went to the Halifax Public Library and searched telephone books, in which I found a listing for a Mrs. Lila Bohaker. I concluded that at her age, this must mean she was widowed or divorced, and thus safer to contact. We also found several Callbecks— our brother Dick's birth surname—listed in Summerside, Prince Edward Island, where his birth mother was from. Several of them were mechanics, just as Dick had been before his death. We went no further with that search. Looking in Moncton phone books for Donna's birth mother was not an option, as we had been told her father was killed before she was born and her mother died shortly after.

With no other avenues open to me, I wrote to Lila Bohaker on Labour Day, 1980. I asked if she would help me find Lila Dakin, my birth mother, and that I was born Janice Elizabeth Dakin on January 6, 1937, in East Chester. I mailed the letter and waited through an intermittent postal strike. Five weeks later, her reply arrived. It was signed, "Love & Kisses— X—Mom." I wouldn't have believed her if she had denied being my mother but still, I was stunned by the reality of her admission.

She was happy I had found her and told me I had two sisters, Joan and Edith. She phoned a few weeks later as my reply was stuck somewhere in the strike. We made plans to meet in July 1981. I asked her who my father was. She said she had promised not to name him, but gave me non-identifying information, including the town he was from. One of my best friends lived in that town, and within minutes I had learned his first and last names. It would be twelve years before I had

Janice

Donna (4 yrs, 9 mos), also born at The Ideal Maternity Home, and sister, Janice (3 yrs, 4 mos)—May 3, 1946.

Janice with birth sisters Edith (L) and Joan (R)—August 1995.

Janice—October 1997.

Easter 1985—Marilyn (birth cousin), Mom Bohaker (birth mom), Janice, Edith (birth sister) and Evelyn (birth aunt).

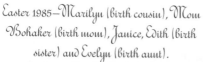

positive proof that the first name was wrong.

My next decision was how, or if, I would tell mom. How could I convince her that I would always be her daughter, and that she would always be my true mom? I decided to shoulder the guilt and spare her the pain of wondering. In July 1981, I was reunited with Mom Bohaker. There were hugs and smiles, but no tears. She asked me to thank my mom for her. We were both nervous until Edith and Joan arrived, and although there was some apprehension, there was also warmth and happiness in our meeting. In the years that followed they told me I was the lucky one.

I was emotionally exhausted by the time I arrived in Digby, and needed the big hug provided by my brother-in-law. I had been on an emotional roller coaster all day and couldn't wait to see mom and hug her. I was more than a little apprehensive that my two mothers lived only twenty miles apart.

Before Mom Bohaker died in 1990, we exchanged many letters. I saw her every year and eventually met cousins, nieces, nephews, and two very special aunts. One I met by chance in my niece's store in Digby one bright sunny day. She was the wife of the man who had signed my Release for Adoption. The other, Auntie Ev, became precious to me very quickly. They were all warm and loving, and totally accepted me as one of the family.

I did not look for my father, but, in 1986, after accidentally seeing the man I thought was him, I wrote to tell him who I was and enclosed a photo. He never saw my letter. His eldest son had the same initials and it was he who phoned me, after going with his sister to question Lila. During their conversation, Lila asked them about their father's cancer. But their father never had cancer. The man's son suggested that, although I looked like one of his sisters, I also looked like the daughter of their father's fourth or fifth cousin. I dropped my quest still convinced that we shared the same father. I could not deny the emotional reaction that shot through my body when I had seen their father and knew immediately who he was, even though I had never seen him before.

The pain that came with reading *Butterbox Babies* was searing. Along with the horror of what happened with babies and mothers, came the knowledge that many of the people we knew while growing up were named in the book for one reason or another—including our adoptive father. The sense of betrayal was staggering. I read about all the adopted children who had been told their mothers had died—I thought about the story my sister had been told, and I wondered.

On December 11, 1992, my phone rang. After verifying who I was and that I had relatives in the Annapolis Valley, a caller identifying himself as Al said, "I'm either your brother or your cousin." He had just found out about the letter I had written to his dad six years earlier. With a pounding heart I told him everything I knew and with the aid of his sister in Halifax we began to unravel the mystery.

While I was savouring this miracle, Donna had one too. A phone call. It was similar to mine—verification of her identity. The caller was a woman who identified herself as Joanne and said, "I think I am your half-sister." Unbelievable! A sibling had never entered our heads, but the greatest miracle of all was that Donna's birth mother, Lola, was very much alive. I was so happy for her. Four days later, she met her sister and her mother and, amid tears and hugs, I met them later that summer. Now her mother has three daughters—me included.

Meanwhile, my "maybe brother and sister," and I were immersed in the effort to prove my birth father's identity. At Christmastime, one of my cousins sent me a photo of my birth mother's family. I wrote to thank her and asked if her mom, Auntie Ev, knew anything that might help me.

Phone calls, information, and photos flew back and forth and just as I was convinced that these two were my brother and sister, a letter arrived from Auntie Ev naming my father. He was not their father; he was the fourth or fifth cousin that had been mentioned to me so long ago. He did have cancer and had died in 1975. The two men had very similar histories. I was close to tears as I called Al, who I now knew was my cousin. He sounded as sad as I felt, but he and his sister remain a very special part of my family. In spite of my sadness, I knew who my father was. My roots were established. That summer I visited with their father and I learned many things about the man who was my father.

My father had a brother to whom I wrote on Father's Day, 1993. He phoned to confirm that I was his brother's child but he was hesitant about telling my sister and four brothers. That summer, on my way back to Calgary from Nova Scotia, I stopped in Ontario and met the woman

I knew was my sister, in the store where she worked. We talked about Nova Scotia. She told me her daughter lived in Edmonton, but I didn't tell her who I was. I was waiting for my uncle to break the news. I waited four months, and at the cost of never hearing from him again, although he was kind enough to send me two portraits of my father, I wrote to my sister. She wrote back, shocked but pleased to have a sister. Not long after, I also talked with two brothers, a niece, and a nephew. It was hard to sleep that night. The other two brothers do not acknowledge me, but I understand that everyone does not react the same way. In 1994, I met my sister, her two daughters, her son-in-law, and granddaughter. She didn't remember meeting me in her store. Last summer they visited me, along with an excited niece, who wasn't supposed to know I existed. We stay in touch but have been careful because her mother is still living.

There are many similarities between me and my two birth families, physically and mentally. The coincidences are amazing. Now I know where our twins "came from." Many Christian names in my adoptive family and my birth families are the same. The husband of a couple who were best friends with Donna and her husband turned out to be my third cousin. And I found I had been in the same classes all through junior and senior high school with a boy who had been named after my birth father.

My journey is complete. I know who I am—totally. Most people understand, some still do not. They say I had a good life, a good mother and father. It is I who do not understand them. Why, when they grew up looking into the faces of their mothers and fathers, can they not understand that I, too, wanted to see those faces, the faces that are reflected in mine?

For all of the pain revealed in *Butterbox Babies*, there is also some joy. If not for its publication, Donna would never have been found by her sister, and I would never have been able to share the joy with her. I hope this joy will come to those still searching. We should also be grateful to Canadian author Mavis Gallant, who paid a price for her early exposé of the Ideal Maternity Home. Over forty-seven years later, I had the unexpected privilege of publicly thanking her on behalf of all Survivors. It was a highly emotional moment for both of us.

Hear Me

Thank you for the love you gave us, thank you for the way you
raised us, thank you for the tears and laughter, thank you,
now and ever after.
Thank you for the sacrifice, thank you for the life advice, thank
you for the best we had—you, our steadfast mom and dad.
Questions left unanswered still of the babies on the hill, in the
sea and God knows where, thanks for saving us from there.
Your love shines back from many places but mostly from our
babies' faces, thanks to you we know they are precious gifts
and shining stars.

The Time Is Right

VIVIAN DORIS ELIZABETH SCHNARE

y name is Vivian and I was born at the Ideal Maternity Home for unwed mothers in East Chester, Nova Scotia on February 23, 1939. My birth name was Kathleen Elizabeth Witt, and my mother's name was either Ruth or Florence Witt.

My adoptive parents were living in the Annapolis Valley, in Nova Scotia at the time of my birth. They were one of many other couples who came to the Ideal Maternity Home because they could not have children of their own. Mom was thirty-nine years old and dad fifty-nine.

My father's nephew already had one eleven-month-old child, when he and his wife had another baby boy. The nephew was sick, and unable to work when the new baby arrived, and they couldn't even afford to buy milk, so they asked mom and dad if they would take the baby and raise him as their own. Fourteen years after they took the child, and raised him and loved him as their own, dad's nephew died, and his wife wanted to take her son back to live with her. Being faced with a difficult situation, mom and dad felt that the only fair thing to do was to let him decide for himself. After many bribes by his natural mother of bikes and other toys, plus the prospect of having a big brother to play with, he decided to move back to Chester with his birth mother and her new husband. Years later, he admitted that moving back was the biggest mistake he had ever made.

My mom had a nervous breakdown after that, but several months later she adopted my brother from the Ideal Maternity Home in East Chester. He was a beautiful healthy baby, about thirteen months old at the time. Following the adoption of my brother, Mrs. Young made another trip to my parents' home in the Valley, this time bringing with her a sickly baby girl—me. Mrs. Young told my parents that I would surely die if I did not have good care, and even then I still might not survive. I was four months old, and weighed only seven pounds. She coaxed my mom and dad to take me, and finally they agreed to do so. They had me almost a year before my dad would even hold me. He always said that he was afraid that I would break. I was so tiny and sickly that mom would wrap me in a blanket, place me on the oven door, sit with me, and pray that I would live.

Vivian (Schnare) Ingles—2 years old.

At the time they took my brother and me, they didn't have the money to legally adopt us. My mom was always afraid that my birth mother would find out that I had lived and would come and take us back. Mrs. Young did not charge our parents any money for us. She was glad to get rid of me, to find me a home and parents who would look after me. I truly believe that otherwise I would not have survived and would have ended up being one of the "Butterbox Babies."

My parents remained in the Annapolis Valley until 1943, then moved back to Chester. I was three years old at the time. My dad was a labourer, and he mowed lawns, dug graves, and also worked for the Youngs for several years as a groundskeeper. When we moved back to Chester, mom and dad bought a house about a five-minute drive from the Ideal Maternity Home.

I was not aware of the scandal that surrounded the Ideal Maternity Home until I was in my early teens. To those of us living in Chester, the Home was just another place, like the grocery store or the flower shop. People knew the building was there, but no one really paid a lot of attention to what was going on. People were involved in their own lives and families, and there was no reason to suspect that anything out of the ordinary was going on at the maternity home. It had been an established business, a part of the community, since 1928. I really believe that the majority of people just took the place for granted. There wasn't a lot of talk about what supposedly went on there, of selling babies or of letting babies die.

I was never a good student in school, and also had a mind of my own. When I was thirteen years old, after the Home had been closed down by the government and reopened as a hotel, I worked for the Youngs. I waited tables, worked in the kitchen, and made beds. The Youngs were really nice people to work for. Mrs. Young was very strict, and Dr. Young did whatever she told him to do. When I was working there, I would slip away whenever I could and go up to the annex, one of the dome rooms— about eight by ten feet. There were hundreds and hundreds of files in the room. There were rows of filing cabinets and full boxes piled two and three feet high. There were files everywhere, in the cabinets, in boxes, and scattered on the floor. Every chance I got, I went through those files, looking and hoping to find the file with my name on it, which I never did. I only wish we had all of those files now.

Mrs. Young was good to me. One day I was helping out in the kitchen, when I was asked to help clean and prepare a large order of strawberries. The only other strawberries that I had ever tasted were the tiny sweet wild ones. While I cleaned, I ate, and ate, and ate, until finally I was covered from head to toe with a massive case of hives. Mrs. Young arrived on the scene, and seeing my predicament, took me upstairs and prepared a warm bath with baking soda, and made me soak until the itching was gone. If she did suspect me of eating most of her strawberries, she never said a word.

With my parents' permission, I quit school in grade five when I was fourteen years old. I moved to Halifax with a girlfriend and went to work at a nursing home. I stayed there for almost two years, and met

Vivian at Survivors' monument—
August 31, 1997.

my future husband. He was twenty-one years old and I was sixteen when we got married. We built a house in Chester, next door to my parents' home. We were married for five years when I was told that I could not have children, so we adopted a beautiful healthy boy. My husband was in the navy for twenty-one years, and after retiring was in business for himself for several years. He is now in the Commissionaire Corps, and in October of this year, we will be celebrating our forty-second wedding anniversary.

My adoptive parents were the most loving and caring people in the world. I was baptized as Vivian Doris Elizabeth Schnare and was married under that name. Because of what had happened to mom before she adopted us, I could never even think of looking for my birth mother while she was still living.

When our son, Harold, was three, my dad died from cancer at the age of eighty-two. My mom stayed in her home, alone, except in the winter or if she was sick—then she would stay with us. In 1981, she was diagnosed with cancer too, and we moved in with her as she did not want to leave her own home. She was with us until she died in 1985.

At school I was called a "bastard," a word I didn't even know the meaning of. I had never been told that I was adopted, so when our son Harold was four years old, we told him that he was adopted. He asked how much he cost, and we told him jokingly, "an arm and a leg." When he was older, we told him that if he wanted to look for his birth mother we would help him. In 1994, he found his birth mother as well as his father and two sisters, all living in Ontario. He turned out to be the most loving son in the world. He never gave us a day of worry. In 1985, he married and now has three beautiful children of his own, Laura, Natalie and Evan. They live only an hour's drive from us, so we see them often.

When I went to get a copy of my birth certificate, I was told that I would have to get a certified copy of my marriage certificate. I was also told that I may not be legally married as I was married under the name Schnare, and not Witt, which was my "real" name. To be legally married, I would have to have my name changed. Later, I was told that I could get my birth certificate under the name of Witt. Now with the changes in the disclosure laws, I have one more visit to make. Because I was never legally adopted in Nova Scotia, I can request and receive my full birth certificate and identifying information. Maybe after all of these years, some of my long-standing questions will finally be answered, and maybe I will learn the part of my story that predates 1939.

In November 1992, at the first Survivors' reunion, I met many wonderful people. Some of them were girls I had gone to school with, and I was never aware that

Vivian and husband, Bob.

they had been born at the Home. It felt like we were one large family. It touched my heart in a way that I can't explain. I would love to meet them all again, but in a place where we could sit around and talk and have a chance to get to know each other a bit better. What a large family I have now—a hundred or more brothers and sisters, especially since out last reunion in 1997. I am anxiously waiting for our next gathering to see all of these wonderful people again.

I have not looked for my birth mother yet, but if it is not too late, the time is right for my search to begin.

I Was a Bought Baby

DENA

It was an unusually warm day in my hometown of Salmon River Bridge, Jeddore, Nova Scotia. I had a list of errands to do, including the usual household chores of banking and grocery shopping. All I could think of was getting these things done and trying out our new pool, which had just been installed on the weekend.

When I arrived home and started to unload my parcels, my daughter, Sara, told me, "Mom, we're getting crank telephone calls." She said that the phone would ring, and after she said "hello" she could hear breathing, and the person would hang up. "I'm not sure," Sara said, "but I think I heard Gramp's voice in the background."

My mother has been deaf as far back as I can remember, and my father has been declared legally blind. Being their only daughter in the immediate area, I do a lot for them; shopping, banking, maintenance and all the other help older people require. I have a younger sister, Deb, who lives an hour or so away, but with two small children she can't really do as much as she would like.

The hardest part of helping out my parents is that all they do is fight with us and complain about me and my family. My mother has accused, abused, and cursed at me all my life, so I'm used to it.

I decided to go to my parents' house to investigate the problem. As I got out of the car at their home, I could hear them fighting with each other inside. "I just wanted to tell you your phone wasn't working properly," I called through the locked door. Now the shouting and cursing was directed toward me. Something in me snapped; I couldn't take this

Dena at 6 months.

Dena at
8 years (1951).

Dena at 17 years .

Dena and David, a fellow Survivor
and friend, at the Survivors'
Homecoming, July 1998.

Elizabeth, Dena and David, David,
and sister Deb (6 years), in front, 1963.

anymore. I said that I wouldn't be coming back again, and, torn with emotion, I got back into the car and drove home.

Later, I called my sister to tell her what had happened. Deb said that she and mom had had a fight the night before, and, as usual, she was taking it out on me.

We couldn't figure out what was happening—our mother's behaviour was definitely getting worse.

The next week, my husband, Dave, said, "Dena, I have to talk to you. It's important."

"What in the world did I do now?" I said jokingly.

"Dena, this is serious," he said. "The Johansens are not your parents. You were a bought baby. You were one of the Butterbox Babies." Everyone in the family knew my history except me, and finally it was my turn. I was shocked; I couldn't believe it. It had never occurred to me that I was an adopted child. That night was a blur—no sleep, no peace, no answers, no mother, no father, and no family.

The next day, my son, Jeffery, arrived after putting both my parents in the hospital. He told me the story that his grandparents told him. The story they were supposed to take to the grave.

My birth name was Maxine Louise Hiltz, daughter of Hilda Hiltz. They didn't know who my father was. My birth mother was forty-two years old when I was born at the Ideal Maternity Home, East Chester, Nova Scotia, on September 22, 1944. On September 28, 1944, when I was six days old and weighed approximately four pounds, two women came to the Home; one was Jean Woods, the other Magdelene Johansen. Magdelene picked out a baby with blue eyes, high cheek bones, and large ears—probably a baby who would pass for the child of Magdelene's husband, who was a tall, blonde, blue-eyed Norwegian. That baby was me. Magdelene took me out of the Ideal Maternity Home and left on the same train from East Chester that she had come into town on. The whole transaction took less than an hour. Magdalene's husband, Joe, who was overseas, agreed to send the $75 for the paperwork. He expected to be killed in the war and figured $75 was a small price to provide his wife with some company after he was gone. He asked that the baby girl be named Dena, after his mother. The baby's second name was Jean, for the woman who had accompanied her mother. Magdelene and Jean then went to New Brunswick to get the papers legalized. After the documents were signed, Magdelene frequently left the baby with Jean while she took advantage of the night life. Eventually, she brought me to her mother's house as I was a very sick and small baby. My grandmother ended up raising me until I was a toddler.

Now I felt like a nobody. My birth mother, whoever she was, threw me away, and my adopted mother threw me out of her house and her life. I had survived my unhappy childhood by building a cement wall. She could hit me all she wanted, or pull my hair or curse at me; it didn't hurt me because I had my wall to hide behind.

The nights were endless; I had so many emotions going through my head that sleeping was impossible. I thought of a baby called Maxine Louise Hiltz laying in a box in a strange room … nobody wanting anything to do with that tiny four-pound innocent child. What did I do to come into the world so unwanted? How can you not love a baby? Who was my mother? I thought she must have been the coldest feeling woman I could ever imagine.

When you are adopted, you really don't have any rights. I was allowed to vote, or go to war if need be, and start a family with my husband. But when you ask the most basic of questions about who you are, you receive answers like, "We can't give you the information unless we have written consent from your parents." I was angry. I was forty-nine years old. I wanted to know. My daughter-in-law helped me fill out an application for adoption disclosure, and I received my first ever birth certificate. Dena Jean Johansen, September 22, 1994, province of Nova Scotia—although they told me I might have been adopted in New Brunswick. We contacted the adoption agency in New Brunswick, and made phone calls to people who knew me and my family. Eventually, I was able to confirm my birth at the Home from a close friend of my adoptive mother; she also knew that the papers had been processed in Saint John, New Brunswick.

Once I knew my birth mother's name and age—Hilda Hiltz, born 1901 in Halifax, Nova Scotia—I was able to find other information about her at the Public Archives of Nova Scotia. By checking through the city directories, I was able to trace her through many years. In 1970, her name disappeared, and by checking funeral homes and cemeteries, I found that a Hilda Hiltz was buried in Camp Hill Cemetery. But I had learned there was another Hilda Hiltz born around the same time. I again contacted my case worker in New Brunswick, and after providing them with my adopted father's signature on the information release form, I learned my mother's full name: Beulah Louise Hiltz.

As with many adoptees searching for their birth families, I was too late to find my birth mother while she was still living. Beulah had died in a car accident on November 9, 1970. She left behind seven children— six boys, and one girl, who would be my half siblings. I did get to meet my Aunt Ethel, a very sweet woman who had wanted to adopt me at birth, but throughout, Beulah had denied that she was even pregnant.

Beulah, who was forty-two years old at the time, had gone away for awhile, with the excuse that she had to have an operation. Ethel then found out that Beulah had gone to East Chester, to the Ideal Maternity Home, to have a baby. After they had found out about the pregnancy, Ethel and her husband, Curtis, went to East Chester to try and get me, but by the time they arrived, I had already been adopted. Beulah gave up all rights to me on October 27, 1944, and my adoption was finalized on November 3, 1944, in New Brunswick. Beulah paid extra to ensure her secret was safe, but a worker at the Home recognized Beulah's picture and told my aunt that Beulah gave up a baby girl, who had already been adopted. Ethel had often thought of me throughout the years, and said she wished that Curtis were alive today to see the little girl that he wanted so desperately, all grown up and finally back home.

When Aunt Ethel and I met for the first time, it was with open arms and eyes full of tears. We shared stories, pictures, and more tears. I also met my first cousin, Marjorie, who also welcomed me with hugs. Aunt Ethel couldn't remember the name of my biological father, but she knew that he was the police chief of Berwick at the time. My search for more of my family continues, and despite the outcome of that search, I give thanks that I have found those I did, and have become one with them.

"Mommie, Come Get Me!"

ROSE WINNIFRED

"Mommie, come get me!" How many hundreds of times did I say those words as a child, and how often have they echoed through my mind as an adult? How many times did I hope and pray for someone to be there for me, someone special, to love me and call me their own? How many times have I thought about the woman who was my mother, and longed to hear her voice and look into her eyes, to hug her and tell her that I loved her?

I was born in July 1942, and never knew my mother. I have no knowledge of those early years that I spent at the Ideal Maternity Home, and have no idea of how long I was there. I do remember standing at a gate and watching people coming and taking babies away. I have often wondered why no one ever wanted me. Maybe it was because I had a strawberry-like birthmark on my face. I was told that it disappeared a few years after a priest blessed it.

I was a toddler when I finally went to live with the family that chose me. Even being chosen, it wasn't my destiny to end up living in the "perfect" family, to enjoy many of the normal joys and milestones of childhood, or to reach adulthood and be able to look back on the good years. The memories that followed me reflected years of confusion, loneliness, and insecurity. There was alcoholism in our home, as well as

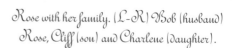

Rose with her family. (L-R) Bob (husband) Rose, Cliff (son) and Charlene (daughter).

Rose and brother Bill (also adopted from the Ideal Maternity Home).

Rose with husband, Bob.

Rose with first birth cousin, Richard (reunited June 1998).

Rose's husband, Bob, with Rose's first birth cousin, Sharon.

domestic violence. I was afraid to go home after school, never knowing what to expect.

My brother, Bill, who was also born at the Ideal Maternity Home, was adopted first, by an older couple who returned a year later to the Home and chose me. We were brought up to know them as our grand-parents. Following their deaths, their daughter, Margaret, took Bill, and their son, Jack, and his wife, took me, though I was never legally adopted. Although we lived in separate houses, Bill and I were raised from the beginning as brother and sister. This was my third set of parents, and I felt I never really belonged to any of them.

There was quite a difference in my parents' ages. When my mother married, she was forty-two years old, while my father was twenty-two. The only good memories that I had as a child were those of growing up with my brother Bill.

As a child, I would get very upset and drop things whenever I was around a lot of noise, so I was only allowed to drink from a cup that was tied to the sink. I rarely received anything that was new from my parents. All my clothes were made by my cousins from my mother's cast-off cloth-ing. To this day, I am only comfortable when I am dressed up.

We lived in Halifax while I was growing up. My family kept chickens, cats, and dogs. When the city would no longer allow farm animals to be kept in the city limits, we moved to Hammonds Plains; I was twelve years old. My mother died when I was sixteen. Following her death, dad told me he wasn't my father, that he and my mother were only "my sponsors." I lived at home until I was eighteen, and then, unable to tol-erate the alcohol and abuse in the home, I went out on my own.

Just prior to my marriage in 1965, I applied for a birth certificate, and was told that there was no birth certificate in my name, Rose Winnifred Sullivan. There was one in the name of Rose Winnifred Walker, but noth-ing to indicate that I was adopted or had the name Sullivan, which I grew up with. My name was listed as Helena Lila Walker on my baptism cer-tificate. I now had three names, and didn't know which was correct—if any of them. I finally got my birth certificate with the last name entered as Walker-Sullivan. This was a compromise to say the least.

My marriage, a mixture of good and bad, only lasted nine and a half years. Four years later, I married my present husband, the man of my dreams, and my life was complete—except for finding my birth family.

I approached the Department of Community Services, but received nothing that would confirm my identity. Parent Finders Nova Scotia eventually contacted someone named Walker, who turned out to be a cousin of mine. Once convinced that my search was genuine, and having determined that their aunt was, in probability, my birth mother, they provided me with her name and telephone number. I had found her at last, and would finally make contact with her.

On April 8, 1998, I heard my mother's voice and spoke with her for the very first time. Unfortunately, at eighty-six years of age, and having already suffered several strokes, she had some difficulty remembering the details of my birth, but as we talked she remembered more.

In addition to finding my mother, I have communicated with many members of my family, and we have begun to share information about ourselves, and to get to know each other. Although my mother has had some health problems, she still lives alone, but is surrounded by many family members who look in on her. At the time of writing, I have just completed making arrangements to travel to Ontario to meet her and other members of my new family.

My husband and I have already gone to New Brunswick to visit my first cousins. When I arrived, it was a homecoming for me. I was welcomed with love and open arms into the family that I had searched for. We shared family histories and photos, and talked about how we could close the gap caused by all those lost years. For the first time, I have met people who look like me, and who, in addition to my children, have the same blood. While visiting with Sharon, my first cousin, she showed me a special chair that had belonged to my grandfather (who I now have pictures of)—it had been his favourite chair. At her invitation, I carefully allowed myself to sit in Grampie's chair. It was almost as if I could feel the warmth of his body, and felt the contentment of being in contact with another member of my family.

When I take that long anticipated step toward meeting my mother, I am prepared for whatever happens. For most of my life, she has been a fantasy that I never thought would become reality. I have found my mother, and already I have a feeling of peace. Whether we have a relationship or not, I will love her, and without judgement. Maybe those cries of "Mommie, come get me!" will finally be silenced from within, and we will still have time to catch up on some of those lost years.

Although we have found each other, I am still frustrated at the barriers that have always been in the way—the secrecy, the lies, and the bureaucratic interference in our lives. Without those, we may have been able to meet much sooner, and she wouldn't have had to wait for fifty-six years to hear me say, "I love you, mom."

For as Long as You Want Me

"But I thought you were dead. What an answer to prayer!" These were the words of my birth mother. It was Thanksgiving 1986 when we were reunited. I had finally found her after years of searching.

I was born in June 1942 in the old Dawson Memorial Hospital, in Bridgewater, Nova Scotia. My birth mother signed a paper she thought was my death certificate. She was actually signing permission for me to go to the Ideal Maternity Home in East Chester and be adopted. Six months later, the sheriff brought me to my new home in Bridgewater. My adoptive mother wanted to send me back because I was tiny, skinny, and frail—not the beautiful plump baby she had hoped for. Perhaps this is why I felt my adoptive father showed me more love than mom or anyone else in the family. We lived next door to dad's parents, but I never felt the same acceptance as the other grandchildren. This may be why I felt so insecure and self-critical. Growing up, I was not abused, but was not treated lovingly. Mom and dad fought frequently, so I didn't feel free to bring friends home to play. The Salvation Army Corps had a Sunday School across the street from where we lived. I felt accepted there; my background, poor clothes, and lack of friends did not seem to matter. As a result, my Christian faith became important to me. I often think how different my life might have been without that love.

I don't remember being told I was adopted—I just knew. After my marriage and the birth of my daughter, I began searching for my roots.

Social Services were no help, as their policy was to not reveal any information. Fortunately, a friend mentioned that a lady in a South Shore community, where my birth mother might have lived, resembled me. She turned out to be my mother's aunt. I gave my friend permission to make inquiries. By chance, she called a woman who had had a child the same week as my birth mother. This woman remembered my birth mother, and knew that her brother still lived on the old homestead, so we showed up on my uncle's doorstep! When he opened the door, he looked shocked at the resemblance. He invited us in, and showed us family photo albums, and told me my birth mother's name, and where she was living. After a week or so, my friend called my birth mother and she agreed to meet me after telling her three daughters. Her husband already knew about my birth. She and I planned to meet at a restaurant the following weekend. When she came through the door, my daughter, who was with me, said, "Here comes your mom." The resemblance was striking. After hugs and conversation, we went outside to meet my stepfather, who welcomed me with tears and open arms. We then went to my younger sister's home, where my family and I were welcomed by everyone. Afterwards, there was a grand gathering at my parents' home. My stepfather, who hoped I would call him "dad," insisted on giving me pictures and keepsakes to take home. On the way home, my daughter, aged thirteen at the time, said, "Mom, I never felt so loved!" Since the reunion, we have always been treated as equals, with no resentment.

My adoptive father died two years before I found my birth family. My adoptive mother was still living, but she never acknowledged my reunion. She died in 1988. We had eight happy years before my birth mother died. How grateful she was to have found me, and I her. My dad's words to me after her death were, "Will you still come?" "For as long as you want me, I'll be here," I replied. Two of my sisters attended the Ideal Maternity Home reunion in Chester in 1997.

My birth mother told me who my birth father was, but I chose not to contact him, since I don't believe he even knew of my birth. Because of the acceptance I felt from my birth mother and family, I did not want to stir up anything from the past that might be hurtful. I am so glad to

Carol with her birth sisters.
(L-R) Olga, Carol, Agnes, and Janet—1986.

Carol (approx. 3 years old)—1945.

First Christmas together—1986. Carol's birth mother,
Carol, daughter Tanya, and stepfather.

Carol with her birth sisters Agnes and Olga at the
Memorial Service in Chester, NS, August 31, 1997.

have met my birth mother and to have a second set of parents and sisters, who have enriched my life beyond description.

When asked what it was like to suddenly discover that she had another sister, Carol's sister Olga responded: "Through the years I have grown closer to my sister Carol, and have found that we are similar in many ways. We have been through many happy, and some very difficult times together. Those included the unexpected death of our mother, and the loss of dad two years later. As a family, we remain in touch and spend a great deal of time enjoying each other's company. I love my sisters and believe we are blessed to have found each other."

Proud to Be a Survivor

DIANNE

y name is Dianne, and I was born at the Ideal Maternity Home in July 1942. I was adopted by a local family, and brought up in Chester, Nova Scotia. Although some people will find this hard to believe, I have pleasant memories of Mrs. Young hugging me and calling me one of her angels.

I was five weeks old when my adoptive grandmother, mother, and sister visited the Ideal Maternity Home. My grandmother, Mrs. Hiltz, and my eleven-year-old sister, Marion, found me in a crib behind a door. They couldn't believe how much I looked like Marion as a baby. Mrs. Young told them I was spoken for and gave them a tour, as there were lots of other babies, but mother wanted me because I looked like Marion. Mrs. Young knew my grandmother very well, so she got permission from my birth mother to let me go to a Protestant home. My birth mother trusted Mrs. Young's decision and let me go. Mother then left me at the Ideal Maternity Home for a week, as she had to go home and prepare for a baby.

The only money involved in my adoption was for the legal costs. Actually, my legal papers were mixed up, and I did not have a proper birth certificate until my sixteenth birthday. Twenty-two months after my adoption, my parents had a son, Robert. He and I were very close growing up. When I was six, tragedy hit our family: our big sister Marion died suddenly at the age of sixteen.

I learned of my adoption when I was eight years old.

It wasn't until I became a teenager that I really understood what

Dianne

Dianne with adoptive brother,
Robert, age 5 years (1947).

Dianne with adoptive sister, Marion.

Dianne, age 25, with her babies—Kathy
(centre) and Sheri (right)—1969.

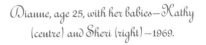

Dianne with her new family, 1946.
(L-R) Clifford Lee, Leola Lee, Marion,
Robert and Dianne (not a happy camper).

adoption meant. I can remember going home very upset that someone had said to me, "You don't even know where you come from."

My father died just before my sixteenth birthday. He was such a kind and gentle person, who used to dance me to sleep as a child.

I can't remember exactly how old I was when I started to wonder about my birth mother. I know I was quite young. For years I tried to find out from the Receiver General who my birth mother was, but got nowhere. One day, Mum gave me a piece of paper she had found among my father's papers. It had my mother's name on it: Dianne Shirley Amero, daughter of Hermeline Amero, born July 27, 1942.

Mum had always said she thought my birth mother came from Digby or Yarmouth. Once I had the name Amero, I searched the phone books, and twenty minutes later I was talking to a lady who was a friend of my birth mother's sister. This lady gave me my birth mother's married name and where she lived. She also told me I had a biological brother. For eight years, I knew where my birth mother lived, and used to phone her and drive by her place many times. No response! Then, one Christmas vacation, I phoned again. This time she asked me where I was. I was only ten minutes away in Halifax. She said her husband was away and she wanted to see me.

I have only spent four beautiful hours with my birth mother, and that was fifteen years ago. Her husband didn't know about me, and she told him I was a family friend. I used to write to her like a friend, and send her pictures of my daughters. I have not had any contact with her for two years.

Dianne with adoptive mother, LeolaLee, and brother, Robert.

When I got married, I told my husband there was one thing I had to do in life—adopt a baby. I wanted to prove Mum wrong. I always felt that she had to have loved Robert more than me because she gave birth to him. She always said she loved us both the same; I found that hard to accept.

As fate had it, I lost many babies myself. In 1967 my husband and I adopted a six-week-old baby girl, Sheri Leigh. One year and five days later, I gave birth to another beautiful baby girl, Kathy Lynn. I'd like to let everyone who's adopted out there know that my mother did not lie to me. Those babies are mine and I could never choose between them.

When I walked my babies down the streets in Chester, people would frequently ask, "Which one is yours?" This made me so angry, and I always said, "They are both mine." I promised my adoptive daughter that when she was nineteen, I would try to find her birth mother.

We all handle adoption differently—for the past five years, my daughter has had no interest in becoming involved with her birth family. I would like to have developed a friendship with my birth mother—I did meet my biological brother, and we have gotten together for a few visits.

Dianne with her new-found birth brother, Murray.

Although I feel that *Butterbox Babies* contains much truth, I don't believe that babies were murdered there; a lot of babies at that time died in hospitals too. I grew up in Chester, and until the book came out, I never knew of anything that went on. As with any small town, stories can be exaggerated. I would like to believe that some good did happen at the Ideal Maternity Home. If you think about it, something good did happen—we all started our lives there, and I'm proud to be a Survivor.

Dianne shared the story of her birth, and her feelings for her adoptive mother, Leola Lee, with her daughter Kathy. Kathy has found her own special way to retell her mother's story and dedicates it, with love, to her mother and her grandmother.

My Angel

In nineteen hundred and forty two,
you found me and I found you.
Fate brought us together that September morn,
at the Ideal Maternity Home where I was born.
Weighing eight pounds four ounces, and five weeks old;
you were given me, I was not sold.
I resembled your daughter, my sister-to-be;
there could be no other, it would have to be me.
There was something about me that caught your eye,
God brought us together, I don't know why.
As I look back over my life and my past,
I treasure the gifts you gave me to last.
You taught me to love all people in life,
including my birth mother for she gave me life.
You taught me respect, including myself,
For all people are equal, no matter the wealth.
I may not have known the roots to my past,
but you let me keep something that truly would last.
My name was Dianne, and it would remain that way,
the only thing I kept from my birth to this day.
I look back on my life with some curious desires;
the same questions we all usually retire.
What did she look like, and what was her name;
why did she do this, there can be no blame.

Mike and Dianne Bone with daughters Kathy and Sheri, at daughter's graduation, 1986.

Leola Lee, Dianne's birth mother — "Her Angel."

For my life has followed a path of its own;
it was not written on paper or cast in stone.
I had a good family with values and love,
what more could a girl ask from God up above.
If anything, you could say I was blessed,
for I had two mothers, one more than the rest.
One who gave me life and my breath,
the other one gave me all the rest.
I dedicate this to my mom, Leola Lee;
for she is the only mother for me.
I love you from my heart, more than words can ever say;
for you were my Angel on that September day!

Kathy Hone

I Have a Complete Past

MARY

ary was another of the Ideal babies who grew up in Nova Scotia. She was born in September 1939. Her birth mother always knew who had adopted her, having been told by Lila Young herself. She had signed a paper, promising never to disturb the family. Lila knew Mary's adoptive mother as well, and had even dated an uncle of Mary's when she was teaching school in Fox Point.

Following her birth, Mary was cared for by her birth mother for six months, and then finally given to the Youngs for adoption. Three months later, her adoptive parents visited the Home and chose her because she said, "Daddy." They also said that they felt sorry for her when they saw one of the nurses slap her for messing up the bedclothes on her cot.

Mary is bowlegged, and has fillings in all her teeth. She has always wondered if this is the result of malnutrition in infancy. Mary was also covered with sores when she was adopted, and had a red birthmark on her shoulder—a potentially life-threatening "defect" at the Ideal Maternity Home.

Mary's search for her birth family began when she was thirty, although family members say that she talked about it at an earlier age. Her adoptive parents told her that the records had been destroyed when the Ideal Maternity Home burned to the ground in 1962. She asked her adoptive parents for any information they might have about her birth parents, and after tearful comments like, "We don't want you hurt by what you find," they offered to find out what they could for her. Her father went to the court house in the town where she had grown up and explained

Mary (1 year old) with her adoptive mom.

Mary (age 5) with brothers David and Peter.

Mary's birth mom, Florence (approx. 25 years old).

Mary with her parents on her wedding day— June 26, 1961.

Mary at high school graduation (15 years old).

Three Generations—daughter, Anne, Mary, and birth mother, Florence.

to a clerk why he was there. The clerk left the room and returned a short time later telling Mary's father that by coincidence, her adoption file was lying on a table in the next room. While the clerk kept busy, her father copied down her birth mother's name and address.

Mary's mother and father then went to the village where her birth mother had grown up, and asked about her at the post office. They were told that she hadn't lived there for years, but that she had a sister, who was staying at her summer home about a mile away. Initially, Mary's aunt refused to provide Mary's birth mother's address, but agreed to ask her sister if she would pass on her address to Mary's mother and father. They later learned that this woman's only child was also adopted.

After much soul-searching, Mary's birth mother agreed to pass on her address. She had not told anyone of Mary's existence, and had guarded her secret well. Later, Mary's parents met with their daughter's birth aunt again, and obtained Mary's birth mother's long-awaited address and phone number, which they sent to Mary. It took her three years to get the courage to call Parent Finders and ask them to make the initial phone call for her. She met her birth mother a month later and they spent two days sharing their stories, pictures, etc.

Mary asked about her birth father. Her mother told her his first name, and that he was married when she met him, and unable to get a divorce, as he was Roman Catholic. She said that one of Mary's sons resembled his grandfather. For her own reasons, Mary's mother was evasive about sharing other details about him. Her birth mother, like many other birth mothers, was hurt my her experience of giving up a child, and is bitter and defensive.

Several years later, when she asked again about her father, her mother gave her his full name and his place of birth. Mary discovered that he was born in a nearby village; she found his birth date, his parents' names, and the names of his siblings. Mary searched in the city directories at the National Archives in Ottawa (available at any local library) and found his name listed in the correct place for the time of her conception. On the advice of Parent Finders, she wrote an open letter addressed to him and sent it to the Old Age Security Pension Department asking that it be forwarded to him. To her surprise, they did, and he answered. She arranged to meet him, using the excuse that she was interested in family history, and was trying to create a family tree. She didn't tell him that she was his daughter, because she had learned that his wife knew about her, and Mary didn't want to cause her any more grief.

Mary and her husband visited her father, and saw that, as her mother had said, he did resemble his grandson. She also learned that she had three half-brothers. She spoke to one of them on the phone, again using genealogy as her reason for calling.

Her birth father's wife has since died, and Mary is considering telling him who she really is, after asking his priest to ask him if he would like to meet someone claiming to be his daughter. If he says no, she can still visit. If he says yes, so much the better. It is interesting that so far, neither her father or half-brother has asked where she fits on their family tree! Mary and her birth family share a talent for music, dancing, and poetry, and an outgoing personality.

Mary also found out that she has two birth cousins. Because of a mental illness in her birth family, her birth mother didn't want her to know about them. But they had a wonderful meeting and are really glad to have found each other. Their mother died when they were young so they were boarded out as children. Mary's birth mother has recently been diagnosed with Alzheimer-like symptoms, so Mary is about to move into another level of knowing and caring for her birth relatives.

Mary was particularly pleased to receive a note of welcome to the clan from the aunt who gave her adoptive parents the name and address that brought about her reunion with her birth parents.

Incidentally, Mary has created a family tree for all four of her birth families, two going back to 1751. She finally has a complete past, and looks forward to meeting more birth relatives, when and if the opportunity arises.

When the Time Is Right

MARGARET

*M*argaret, born on December 25, 1943, remained at the Ideal Maternity Home until she was five months old, when she was adopted by a Nova Scotia couple. Her parents also adopted an eighteen-month-old boy from the Home. Margaret's brother, Jerry Malcolm Gregory, was born on July 14, 1942. Both children felt that they were fortunate to have been adopted by such wonderful and loving parents. In 1969, at the age of twenty-six, Jerry was killed tragically in a car accident. He had never married, and had no knowledge of his birth parents. The family was devastated. Margaret is hopeful that one day she will be able to find some of Jerry's family to share information about her brother with them. Their dad passed away in 1988, and their mother in February 1998.

Margaret and brother, Jerry (also adopted from the Home).

Margaret doesn't know if there were costs attached to their adoption. Their adoptive parents told them very little about their adoption or the Home they came from. One day, when Margaret was about ten years old, a playmate told her and Jerry that their mother and father were not their real parents. Of course, they didn't believe it. They expected their parents to deny the story, and it was only then that they were told the truth. Even when they became adults, their parents didn't want to talk about the adoptions or the Home. Neither child had ever seen their adoption papers, and Margaret has no idea what happened to them. She was told that

Margaret (left) and playmate.

her parents kept the names she and her brother were given at the Home, but when at sixteen she received a copy of her birth certificate, the name "Fern," rather than Margaret, was on it. She had been named Fern Elizabeth by her birth mother. She had since had her first name "Margaret" legally added to the others.

Unlike many others from the Home, Margaret has met her birth mother several times. Her mother first looked her up when Margaret was about eleven years old. She has also met her maternal grandparents and one uncle, all of whom have since died. Her mother is still living in Ontario, and they do communicate occasionally, although they haven't seen each other for more than twelve years.

Her mother told her that she was living in Halifax when she became pregnant. After Margaret was born, she went to Ontario and got married. Ironically, she later discovered that she could not have any more children, so she and her husband adopted two. Her mother also told her about her stay at the Ideal Maternity Home. She said that Mrs. Young was very good to her, as she was to most of the girls there. She also said that she helped with the babies while she was there, and that she was occasionally told to feed some of the babies only water and sugar, because they were sick and couldn't keep anything down. Everyone did as they were told.

Margaret knows very little about her father, except that his name was Garnet Earling Hicks, and that he was a sick-bay attendant in the navy at the time of her conception. His home was in Belleville, Ontario. Only after she became pregnant did Margaret's mother find out that he was married with three children. There is still a chance that some day

Jerry

Margaret may find her father and three half-siblings, which will open a new chapter in her life. Right now, even though she does have a couple of possible telephone numbers, she still hasn't gotten up the courage to call and open up this door.

Chosen, Adopted, and Loved

Janette, who was born on December 10, 1944, only remained at the Home for three weeks before being chosen and adopted by her parents. Her mother answered an advertisement in the *Halifax Herald* that advertised "Babies For Adoption." She applied, and received a call to come to the Ideal Maternity Home. She took the train to Halifax and then to East Chester, where she was met by Dr. and Mrs. Young, who were very hospitable. They gave her a room and supper, then took her to see the babies.

Janette at 4 years old.

Janette was the first baby that was shown. She was in a separate room from the others, and her mother examined her to make sure she was in perfect condition. Dr. and Mrs. Young tried to convince her to adopt Janette, but her mom became upset by their insistence because they were not letting her make a choice. She told the Youngs that she would like to see some of the other babies and was taken to a dormitory-type room with a lot of cribs and beds. When she went into the room she was met by a young woman holding a small baby, who came up to her and asked her to "Please adopt my baby." The baby had a heart problem. At the same time, a little boy ran up to her and asked her to take him home. One of the girls who looked after Janette and was dressed like a nurse, showed Janette's adoptive mother a picture of Janette's birth mother and told her that she had left the Home a few days ago. Janette and her new mother left the next day to begin a new life. The only money that her adoptive mother paid was $25 in legal fees, but she felt that the Youngs were well paid because they pushed so hard to have Janette adopted.

Janette has lost both of her parents now, but is thankful that they gave her a wonderful life. She knew that she was adopted from an early age, and wouldn't have changed the parents she had under any circumstances. She was loved and cared for, and her parents gave her lots of attention. They already had a child of their own, but wanted to adopt a little girl. Although Janette considers herself very lucky, she still has questions that she wants answered.

Janette was born Mary Nancy Langille, daughter of Jean Langille. When she wrote to the Department of Community Services for information, she learned that her mother was a student nurse and a Roman Catholic. Her birth father was in the navy.

She attended the Memorial Service in Chester, Nova Scotia in 1992, with her husband and her mother. She happened to speak with Reverend Crowell of the Lunenburg parish, who told her that she looked familiar. On her way home it occurred to her that she may resemble someone in his congregation. Apparently, her birth mother was from the South Shore area. It was an eerie feeling to think that her birth mother, or aunt or uncle, could be in the Reverend's parish.

Janette, with Bob Bartlett, following the dedication of the monument to the babies of the Ideal Maternity Home, August 31, 1997.

A Good Chance
at a Good Life

June celebrates her birth date as July 6, 1933, although she thinks her mother may have changed the dates of her and her sister's births, because she didn't want people to know they were adopted. She has no information about her birth parents, other than that name may have started with a "P" or "B."

Her parents were wonderful people, who gave sick babies from the Ideal Maternity Home a good chance at a good life. Altogether, June has four siblings that came from the Home. Her parents had taken two boys from the Home in 1939 or 1940, but they died. A year or two passed, and they took two more children, who were twins. One of these children also died and there was an inquiry into his death, but the coroner's jury found the death was due to natural causes. Dr. Ralph Smith stated in the coroner's report that the child had died from an infection of the middle ear and blood poisoning. So three out of four children that the couple had adopted from the Ideal Maternity Home died within eighteen months. Their adoptive parents had taken them despite their ill health and had even paid $25 for the transportation from East Chester to Amherst for the last two children. The jury recommended that conditions at the maternity home be investigated.

June has had no luck in obtaining information about herself and her birth family. Her father was apparently a World War I veteran, but there was little information in his files. She did receive his medical files from the Public Archives in Ottawa, but they did not have his personal files. Social Service records don't date that far back, and the Veteran's Pension Board told her that most records were destroyed or lost. Among her mother's personal papers, she found correspondence to the Canada Pension Commission, stating that all children were adopted, but there were no copies of birth certificates. Throughout her search, June has only found closed doors, but still hopes that someday one of these doors will open to allow her to find some of the answers she has been searching for.

I Was One of the
Fortunate Ones

JOYCE

oyce was born at the Ideal Maternity Home on February 14, 1934. She thinks that she was one of the most fortunate of all the babies, as her birth mother, Valence Dexter, was the first registered nurse employed at the Home (in 1933). She took care of Joyce herself until she was eight months old and then she was put up for adoption. She was chosen by a couple from Liverpool and was legally adopted on May 22, 1936. Joyce has an advantage over many of the babies of the Home, as she is fortunate to have several photographs of herself as a baby with her birth mother. While working at the Home, Valence met her future husband, Aubrey Murphy, who was employed as a handyman, and on January 25, 1936, they were married. Things couldn't have been too good at the Home, as Valence was involved in a court case in 1936, and testified against Dr. and Mrs. Young. Shortly after this, she and her husband Aubrey left the Home. When asked about what went on at the Ideal Maternity Home during those years, all she would tell Joyce was "I don't know." Despite her refusal to talk about it, Joyce felt that something bothered Valence all her life.

Joyce knew nothing about the Home until the 1992 publication of *Butterbox Babies*. After being made aware of the Home, she called her aunt, who confirmed that Joyce was born there. At that time, she also

Joyce at Summerville Beach, Queens Co., N.S.

Joyce with her birth mother,
Valence Dexter, while at the
Ideal Maternity Home.

Valence Dexter (R.N.), the first registered nurse
at the Ideal Maternity Home, with her future husband,
Aubrey Murphy, and William and Lila Young
and their son, on the grounds
of the Ideal Maternity Home (approx. 1934).

Joyce, her birth brother Richard,
and birth mother Valence,
at first meeting in 1952.

phoned her birth mother, who still maintained she knew nothing about what went on there.

Joyce had a happy life until her parents started to quarrel when she was about ten years old. They eventually divorced when Joyce was fifteen. After they parted, Joyce maintained contact with her mother, but lived with her father until her marriage in 1953; it was with his help that she managed to find and meet her birth mother.

Although at first she didn't like the idea of meeting her birth mother, when Joyce was eighteen, they were finally reunited. Joyce didn't ask her birth mother any questions, and her mother didn't volunteer any information, except that she couldn't look after Joyce when she was born. Joyce was happy just to meet her mother and half-brother, Richard, and feels compassion for her mother: "It must have been hard for her; she had so many pictures of me as a baby. I know when the book (*Butterbox Babies*) first came out I was shocked to read my mother's name and her husband's (not my father). I wonder how many babies she helped deliver. I sure would like to know. All she says is she doesn't know anything. If she would only talk."

Valence passed away in March 1998, and with her went all of her memories of those years at the Ideal Maternity Home, except for the ones of her daughter, Joyce, who was born there, and her son, Richard, born shortly after she and her husband left the Home.

Journey of Emotion and Liberation

RIVA

am one of the many babies who left the Ideal Maternity Home and Canada for the United States. I was adopted by a childless Jewish couple from Newark, New Jersey. William and Lila Young, the proprietors of the Ideal Maternity Home, had advertised heavily in that area during the 1940s. My mother was one of the many women who travelled to East Chester in search of a baby. My father did not accompany her. I could never understand how such a momentous decision as selecting a child could be so unilateral. I was four months old when I left Nova Scotia, and fifty-two years passed before I returned.

Although I was told at an early age that I was adopted, the underlying message was that the topic was off-limits. My parents provided only cursory details, which I would later learn were inaccurate. For most of my life, the subject of my adoption was a very difficult one to discuss with my mother, and she never initiated the conversations. I can't remember ever talking to my father about it. I only found out recently that the reason my father severed his relationship with his mother was because she couldn't accept me and referred to me as a "momzer" (a Yiddish term meaning bastard).

Yiddish was the second language in our home. My maternal grandmother, a truly wonderful woman who had emigrated from Russia (and who shared my bedroom for twenty-one years), spoke both Yiddish and

English. The adults spoke Yiddish when they didn't want me to understand, though I eventually gained a working knowledge of the language.
Although I was raised by Jewish parents in a predominately Jewish neighbourhood, I never attended a synagogue or was forced to go to Hebrew
School, which was two days weekly after public school, like the rest of
the kids. I had always attributed that to my parents' limited resources
and inability to pay for the tuition. Nevertheless, it was understood that
they preferred that I have Jewish friends and, of course, eventually, a
Jewish husband. It wasn't until my first son, Steven, made his bar mitzvah
(a Jewish confirmation at age thirteen) that I understood. My mother
thanked me for having the bar mitzvah party because I "didn't have to."
That's when I realized that she had never thought of me as Jewish.
According to Talmudic law, a Jew is one who is born to a Jewish mother.
If the mother isn't Jewish, neither is the child. That's why I had never
been given any religious training. Perhaps she knew that I had been
baptized on the day of my birth, a fact that I became aware of only
recently. It's no wonder l felt isolated and uncomfortable. It's also no
wonder I always seemed to gravitate toward Christian friends.

It seemed like I always had a strong desire—a yearning—to know more
about my heritage. Of course, the pervasive secrecy only intensified the
curiosity about my past. From time to time, I would search through the
house for clues to my identity. Finally, when I was a teenager, I located the
blue cardboard folder that contained my adoption papers. Now I had not
only my birth name, but also that of my birth mother!

Over the years, I contemplated searching for her, but felt that it would
be disloyal to my adoptive parents, and I knew that I couldn't ask them
for help. So I did nothing. However, after the birth of my first two children, I realized that this genealogical and medical information was not
only my entitlement, but theirs as well. I discussed my increasing need
to know about my heritage with my (then) husband but he discouraged
it and I dropped the idea. In retrospect, I can't believe that I wasn't
more assertive. This wasn't his call, it was mine and mine alone.

In 1977, after vacillating for many years, I finally decided to pursue my
search surreptitiously. I began by obtaining a copy of the Halifax/
Dartmouth telephone book. I sent letters to every person with my birth
mother's last name. My ex-husband was an attorney and I used the legal

stationery that listed our home address. I figured that this would make
the letters seem more official. Also, I felt that my birth mother might
respond in the hope that she was the beneficiary of an inheritance.

Because the letters and envelopes had to be individually typed (this
was before the days of computers) and because I had a full-time teaching position and two young children, I was only able to process a few
letters each day. I became obsessed with the search. Every day I raced
home from work to check for any responses and to type a few more
new letters. Fortunately, it only
took about seventy letters before I
had a response. One day, a woman
telephoned and asked for "the
lawyer." I knew immediately who
she was. Somehow, I managed to
remain calm, and pretended that
I was the legal secretary. I told her
that the attorney was not in the
office, but that if she would give
me her name, address, and telephone number, he would get
back to her. I immediately drove
to my husband's law office and
confessed to my recent activities.

Riva (Barnett) Saia
(approx. 9–12 months old).

He promptly called the woman and announced that he was representing a client who was an adoptee searching for her birth mother. She
confirmed that she had given up a child for adoption in 1945. She
replied to the two follow-up letters in a business-like manner. After
several months, I got up the nerve to telephone my birth mother and
identify myself not only as the attorney's wife, but also as her daughter.

Her attitude was decidedly not what I would consider motherly. She
begged me not to tell her family of my existence because "this has been
a deep secret buried within me all these years and I don't wish to reveal
it at this stage in my life." Although I believe that she has deprived me
of the right to know part of my family, I have honoured that request to
this day. What was even more upsetting was that I had an older brother,
whom she had kept! Unfortunately, he died as a result of an accident at

age six (about three years after she had given me up for adoption). As I recall, our phone conversation was almost surreal. It certainly did not unfold as I had expected or hoped, particularly since I was her sole surviving child. She did ask for photographs of my two children but I couldn't overcome my hurt and disappointment and decided that if she didn't want me, she couldn't have them. I became bitter, and retreated. She changed residences and left no forwarding address.

However, she had told me my birth father's name. I re-activated my letter-writing campaign and located him after only twenty or thirty letters. He was ninety-five years old at that time, and I was thirty-two. My birth father acknowledged knowing my mother and that he had been her employer years before. He also said that she had had two children, one "a little boy that died." I realized then that he knew about me. I wondered how he knew about my brother's death. Unfortunately, he denied paternity. As a result of that denial, I decided not to pursue my contact with him.

Eleven years later, in 1988, I received an extensive newspaper article from the *Montreal Gazette*, which detailed the story of the Ideal Maternity Home, and the atrocities that were allegedly committed there. I mailed a copy of that article to my (adoptive) parents, who had retired and were living in Florida. My mother confirmed that this was the orphanage that she had dealt with. But, once again, little additional information was provided.

In 1997, twenty years after the initial contact with my birth mother, I decided that if I was ever going to meet her, I had better act soon. I no longer knew where she lived, or even if she was alive. So, once again, I resorted to mailings. By then I knew where her Nova Scotia relatives lived, so locating her was relatively simple. I sent out letters stating that I was an old friend who had lost contact with her. My search was successful. She telephoned me, and about three years ago we met for the first (and probably the last) time. She acknowledged that the meeting was not easy for her, partially because I looked liked the man who denied paternity. Nevertheless, it was a pleasant meeting. Although she opened up a bit, I felt no real warmth between us. One of her puzzling questions was "How old are you?" I had thought that my date of birth would have been etched in her memory forever. Her statement, "I didn't know you were born in Canada," was even stranger. After I responded, "Don't you remember? You were there," she giggled.

Although it was difficult for her to discuss this part of her life, she told me that during the early stages of her pregnancy she lived with my father's sister-in-law. It was his sister-in-law who made all the arrangements with the Ideal Maternity Home, where my mother remained, in a private room, for the duration of the pregnancy. My brother had been delivered by Cesarean section and so was I. She referred to Dr. Young by his middle name: "Dr. Peach wanted to operate, but I said that I wanted to go to the hospital." Fortunately for both of us, she prevailed and I was delivered by Dr. MacDonald at the Grace Maternity Hospital in Halifax. She returned to the Ideal Maternity Home to recuperate. "They weren't anxious to discharge me because they were getting paid by your father," she explained. "They were getting money from your father all along until you were adopted. Your father was so sorry. He said, 'Whatever I wanted to do,' but what was I going to do with two children?"

Riva age 9 months to 1 year, 1945.

In the summer of 1997, a close friend called and told me there was a movie on television that she thought was about the orphanage where I had been adopted. I watched *Butterbox Babies* intently, and learned that the movie was based on the book by Bette Cahill, which I later ordered from a Nova Scotia bookstore. In the meantime, another good friend checked out the Ideal Maternity Home website and made contact with Bob Hartlen. Soon after, I met with six other New Jersey residents who had similar beginnings. Our New Jersey group has now expanded to approximately twenty-five as a result of the local publicity. For the first time, I have an opportunity to share mutual concerns, emotions, issues, frustrations, and the deep need to know my roots. These other adoptees understand and validate my search. Previously, these feelings were relegated to my own private world. The bond of our mutual experience is incredible.

When I made plans to return to Nova Scotia for the Ideal Maternity Home reunion last summer, I decided to re-open my search for paternal relatives. I located my birth father's obituary, contacted the cemetery where he is buried, and asked for the names of his next of kin. I was given the name of a paternal cousin in Tatamagouche, Nova Scotia. I met with her, her husband, and three of their four daughters last August. My cousin knew my mother and had been aware of her pregnancy. In fact, my birth mother had stayed with my cousin's widowed mother for a brief time during those months prior to my birth. They also confirmed that I looked like my father, sounded like him, and laughed like him. At last I had confirmation of my paternal heritage. I also learned that he had a son living in Alberta.

I contacted my brother in Alberta, and he and his wife encouraged me to visit. I flew there last January and was welcomed with open arms. My brother hosted a large family reunion and I was given gifts, and a genealogical chart. Several relatives even thanked me for taking the time to locate them! It was an incredible and emotional experience, much different from the reception I received from my birth mother, who seems to have disappeared once again. Unfortunately, another brother and a sister had passed away by the time I located my family.

I have had a good life and I realize that I was very fortunate to have been chosen from the roomful of babies at the Ideal Maternity Home. Every morning when I look at the LaHave Creamery butterbox that I found in a Nova Scotia antique shop last summer, I contemplate what might have been. I think about the many babies that did not survive and I am reminded of my blessings. I will always be thankful that my birth mother chose adoption in lieu of abortion. I am extremely indebted to my (adoptive) parents and to my maternal grandmother for nurturing and loving me, and for providing me with good values and a fine education. I have been blessed with three wonderful children (Steven, Ellen, and Michael), and my husband, Charlie, has been extremely supportive throughout this venture. I have had a fulfilling career in education, both as a teacher and as a school social worker. Also, I'm very appreciative of the opportunity to meet my birth family members and am hopeful of maintaining lifelong relationships. Only a few months ago, I shared all of my search results with my (adoptive) mother. She has been incredibly accepting of the entire experience. In fact, she has asked me to accompany me and my husband on our next trip to visit what she calls my "other family." This openness has greatly contributed to an improved relationship between us. I am delighted that I found the courage to share the information with her. Finally, there are no more secrets! I believe that I am a mosaic, and that the pieces they all contributed have helped to create what and who I am.

I guess that adoption makes one introspective. Being an only child left me lonely and isolated during my formative years. The limited information about my background created insecurity and a lack of identity. The issues of rejection and abandonment, which had been dormant for years, erupted during my divorce after twenty years of marriage. I have learned a great deal about myself during this journey. It has been an emotional roller coaster but also a very liberating experience. Feelings that I've repressed for years have recently been validated by other adoptees. I have also begun to understand the demons that plagued both my birth mother and my adoptive parents. My recent research has enhanced my appreciation and love for my parents. I am still absorbing the impact of all that has transpired in the last year, yet I know that I have become a more complete person as a result of this genealogical expedition, and I am so delighted that I ventured down this path.

Riva

A Marvellous Life
... and I Cherish It

RITA McGURK

J was born at the Ideal Maternity Home on September 24, 1944. My birth name was Carol Ann Harris and my mother was Annie Robena Harris. I was adopted in April 1945, by a Jewish couple from New Jersey. My parents made it clear to me from my earliest days that I was adopted, and shared the information they had about my birth. In retrospect, it was the wisest thing they did for me. They also made it clear that the reason I had been adopted was to ensure they would have someone to care for them in their old age. To people of their generation, this was not an unreasonable expectation.

Many Survivors speak of the fine families that took them in despite the harrowing circumstances under which their adoptions took place. My adoptive parents went to Canada because no reputable agency in America would give them a child. My mother was almost fifty years old, and suffered from several chronic diseases; my father, although healthy, was the same age. Despite some very difficult years, and the death of my mother when I was thirteen years old, I not only survived, I flourished. In 1976 I decided to search for my birth family. I carried out the project with the help of friends. I encountered sealed records and bureaucratic intransigence. Through a stroke of real luck, and the direction of the people at Parent Finders, I was put in contact with a social worker in Halifax who knew the whole story of the Home. She

Rita at 11 years old.

Rita at 1 year old.

Rita with her family. (L-R) Bob,
Rachel, Rita, and Ryne.

secretly, and illegally, searched the records and found enough information about my birth to get me started.

On learning my mother's name, I obtained phone books from Halifax and Lunenburg County, and wrote a form letter to every person in
every book that had her family name. There were about two hundred.
Eventually I received a letter from a woman who said she thought she
might have information for me. I called her, and when I told her the
details of my story, she said that I was, indeed, her sister's child. Evi-
dently my mother had been one of sixteen children. When her siblings
received copies of my letter, they naturally shared them with the rest of
the family and the whole story came out.

Unfortunately, my mother had died in 1976, but my aunts invited
me to visit them in Shelburne, which I did. The visit was extremely
successful in terms of satisfying my curiosity, but I have never felt the
need to go back. Through my aunts I learned I had two sisters and a
brother, with whom I eventually corresponded. Over the past twenty
years, I have become very close to my sister in Spokane, Washington. I
do not communicate with the other family members.

Mysteriously, my birth mother always admitted to my sister that she
had an older child, but she said that it was a boy, and that he had died.
However, the picture that she kept by her all her life was undoubtedly
of me. In fact, my adoptive mother had a picture of me taken shortly
after that one and in it I'm wearing the same outfit. My adoptive mother
said that when she went to the Home, the Youngs urged her repeatedly
to take two children—me and an older little boy, but she had no interest in him and he was left behind.

Who am I today? My name is Rita McGurk, maiden name Bendett,
raised in Newark, New Jersey. I live in South Yarmouth, Massachusetts,
in the centre of Cape Cod. I have been a registered nurse for over thirty
years and recently completed my Ph.D. at Cornell University. Currently,
I teach psychiatric nursing at the local community college. I share my
life with my husband of twenty-seven years. We have a biological son,
an adopted daughter, and a marvellous life. None of it was purchased
cheaply, and that may be why I cherish it so much.

Our Strength
Is in Our Love

NATALIE

J was born on September 26, 1943, at the Ideal Maternity Home in East Chester, Nova Scotia, and for the first two years of my life I was known by my birth name, Helen. I had a heart condition, and was considered a poor health risk—not a prime candidate for adoption. As I grew older, I became less and less desirable, with people wanting to adopt newborn babies. I was fortunate when, despite my age, an older professional Jewish couple from Newark, New Jersey, adopted me in August 1945. I was given a new name by my parents. My dad was a lawyer, and my mom taught school. I grew up as an only child and led a privileged life. My adoptive parents were devoted to me and treated me wonderfully. My life was filled with love and kindness. I wanted to grow up, get married, have lots of babies, and, without question, adopt a child and give it the kind of chance at life that I had. I did grow up, got married, and after three years adopted a baby boy. Three years later, we adopted a baby girl, and our family was complete. I could not have been happier; my children, to me, were the two most beautiful babies ever created.

I always knew that I was adopted, but we did not spend much time discussing it. I guess it was a sign of the times. I didn't ask a lot of questions and I wasn't given a lot of information. I did daydream frequently, and created a fantasy birth mother. I was the youthful indiscretion of the Queen of England. When things weren't going well at home, I would dream about her. Despite all of my musings, I never thought about searching for my birth mother. This would have qualified as a treasonous act against my parents. Whenever the thought occurred to me, I would feel guilt-ridden and dismiss it.

Last summer, after her twenty-seventh birthday, my daughter Amy told me, "Mom, I've decided that I need to search for my birth mother. I know this is going to hurt you a lot, but I really have to do this...I would like to know if you can help me...do you have any information?" Both of my children were adopted privately, and I did have information that would help, but I denied having it at the time. We talked about it for hours, and all I could do was give her the cons, not the pros, because I honestly thought that there were no pros. I told her she was "playing with fire," that it was a dangerous thing to do, and that she needed to protect herself if she went ahead. "Make sure that you have an intermediary, that you don't just go knocking on doors, or calling people," I said. "You have no idea at what point these people are in their lives, what they know or don't know; you could be affecting a marriage." When I told my husband I had withheld information, he said I had to give it to her, which I did. We both cried a lot, she thanked me and told me that she loved me, and that she would protect herself, and that was that. The next morning she sent me flowers—for the first time in her life.

Amy called an organization called the Seekers of the Lost, and within two weeks they had found her birth mom. Actually, they first found her birth brother. She called him and identified herself, and learned that he did know about her. He said that he would call her birth mother and tell her, and see what she wanted to do about it.

A couple of days later, in August 1997, Amy and her husband went to meet her birth mother. I was terrified. I thought my daughter was walking out of my life. I couldn't stop crying

Amy's birth mom is only sixteen years older than Amy, and they look exactly alike. The reunion was a wonderful, difficult, and emotional event. Amy has a younger sibling, who also has had some adjustments to make after being raised as an only child. Amy has been introduced and welcomed by the family. She has recently found out about her birth father as well, and has been introduced to his family.

When I met Amy's birth mother last October, I told her that I had feared meeting her for twenty-seven years. We both survived the meeting. Now that we have met several times, I feel very differently about her and think that she is wonderful.

In October, I approached a private investigator, at Amy's prodding, to begin my own search. I didn't have a lot of information. I went to the Children's Aid Society in Morristown, and they made inquires in Canada and gave me additional information. They told me that my birth date had been changed and that I was the third child born to my birth mother. My parents had told me that my mother had died shortly after my birth, and that my father, a pilot, had been killed in the war.

By now I wanted to find my birth mom so badly. Seeing how wonderful and positive it was for Amy made this possible. Meeting and talking with other birth mothers who wanted to find their children was a new concept to me.

The investigator called me soon after, and told me that he had good news and bad news. My mother had died in 1986, but she had had another son after I was born. I was devastated that my mother was dead. For me, she died that day.

Three weeks passed and the investigator suggested we contact my siblings, who had been told about me. I didn't want to meet them. I had never been anyone's sister. Finally, the investigator brought photos to show me of my siblings—one sister and three brothers.

I called all four of them, and spent the whole day, into the evening, talking to my brothers and sister. They were all wonderful. They told me about a letter that my adoptive mother had written to my birth mother when I was a little girl. It was sent through an attorney. The letter established my contact with my family. My sister had found the letter when she was ten years old, but had never questioned her mother about it. My older brother had also found the letter. When my birth mom passed away, the letter was near her. She must have read it shortly before she died.

My sister came to visit me for a week, on the July 4th weekend. It was the scariest time of my life. I couldn't believe that she was real. Because my children are adopted, I had never seen anyone who would be like me, someone who shared my blood. It was so exciting but also frightening.

I bought her a welcoming bouquet of flowers and put them in the guest room with a card. When she arrived, I was afraid to hug her, it was all so formal. I felt totally inept, but we got through dinner, and we talked and it was wonderful. While she was there, the meeting day for my support group in Morristown came, and she agreed to come to the meeting. We spent Sunday with my daughter and her husband, and went out to dinner. The next day, I told her that I was seeing a therapist, and had an appointment. I asked her to come with me. She did, and was wonderful. All this time, I was afraid to have any physical contact with her—I didn't hug her or touch her, although I desperately wanted to. I also wanted to tell her how much she meant to me and that I loved her, but was afraid of frightening her away. The day before she left, we went shopping, and she suggested we go to a china shop or a jewellery store and buy a little gift for each other; something to say we would never separate again. We went to the jewellers and she insisted on buying two heart necklaces. They were just so perfect. I was shaking so badly, I couldn't even put mine on, and she said, "It appears that my little sister is so nervous that she can't even dress herself, so I will just have to put it on for her." I felt so small and so loved, just like a child—it was wonderful. It was a turning point.

She went with me to buy my daughter a birthday card. I told her that Amy was spending her birthday with her birth mother this year and that I was really unglued by it. My own sister helped me buy a card for my daughter. It was such a beautiful thing.

The day she left, I hugged her and hugged her, and she let me, but I still couldn't tell her that I loved her, or how important she was in my life. I felt very sad. The next three nights I slept in her bed, and cried and cried. It was my time with my sister.

The private investigator that I had hired told me he had information about where I was born, and gave me the book *Butterbox Babies*. It told of a terrible history and circumstances, of baby trafficking and baby deaths. Later, I was notified that the Survivors and Friends of the Ideal Maternity Home were having a reunion. I booked a flight, made hotel reservations, and the next thing I knew, I was there—and so were my brothers and sister. One of my brothers from Prince Edward Island drove eight hours to spend two with me, and another drove another six to seven hours from New Brunswick. My other brother, who lives in Nova Scotia, acted as our tour guide, and looked after us while we were there. They were fantastic.

The reunion consisted of a Friday afternoon reception of Survivors and Friends, complete with media. It was amazing. Saturday night there was a performance of the play *Aftermath* at a community playhouse in Chester. It dealt with the stories of some of the Survivors, and was powerful and heavy stuff. After the performance, I wrote my thoughts in a journal I kept of my time in Canada: "So hard to watch, so hard to hear. Feelings of being a wee little bastard keep resurfacing. Babies lying in cribs in urine and feces, with flies swarming around them. All the windows closed, one person taking care of eighty babies, not going out of doors to play, not learning to walk, to talk, to play, to eat, to respond appropriately, being almost like Helen Keller." My poor health suggests that I had been treated that way. As far as I know, I lived at the Home for two years before I was adopted. My parents had told me that I was slow. Today they would call it failure to thrive.

There was also a memorial service and a church service. Here I was, a little Jewish girl taking her four protestant siblings to church. The memorial service was totally overwhelming and gut wrenching. In the afternoon, a monument was dedicated to all the babies who had lived in the Home.

While in Canada, I received a gift from my brother. It was a picture of the town that I should have grown up in, with street maps and brochures, and an open invitation to return. There was also a card enclosed that read, "I have never experienced feelings like this before, so intense that they are almost overwhelming. I know we have only known each other for a short time, but you have caught me with my defenses down and have captured my heart, before I knew what was happening. Ever since that moment my days have been filled with thoughts of you and a happiness that keeps me skipping off the ground. Love Ken."

There is another verse on a card, available in the meeting room of my support group, that reflects the feeling of the searcher: "When I first saw you, I was afraid to meet you. When I first met you I was afraid to like you. When I first liked you, I was afraid to love you. Now that I love you, I am afraid to lose you."

That is where it is for me.

When I returned from Canada, it was like a crash landing. I couldn't function and I couldn't work. Although there are still many questions, I feel like a hand in a glove with my family. There is such a strong connection; my attachment to my sister is incredible.

My son, David, started his search this spring. His situation is different, however, from Amy's, as he lives in California and his birth mother is here on the east coast. He has seen his birth mother only once so far, but communicates with her on a regular basis. It was a positive meeting for them.

When we were visiting the site of the Ideal Maternity Home, my sister and I had different reactions. She cried because her mother had gone through this awful experience alone. I was yearning to be with my mother—to touch her, kiss her, feel her warmth and love, hear her voice. I wanted to lie next to her and sleep peacefully as only a child can sleep when she is encircled in the warmth and safety that is Mommie. My feelings are so primal that I am afraid of myself. Wanting to know her pain, to share it and to help ease it.

My sister did not discount my feelings in any way; she was very respectful of where I was. I think we have a great future together. We are family.

A Family Reunited

y adoption was never a secret. The story of how my adoptive mother travelled from New Jersey to Nova Scotia and chose me from the many infants at the Ideal Maternity Home was always one of my childhood favourites. I never questioned my mother's account of my birth family. I had been told that my birth father had been killed in the war and that my birth mother had decided to give me up for adoption rather than raise a child alone. Although I sometimes thought about my birth parents and wondered what they were like, or if I looked like them, I never felt the need to search for my birth mother. I was an adored only child, doted on by parents, grandparents, aunts, and uncles. As a young child, I often wished for a sibling—always an older brother; never a baby brother or sister.

As I grew older, my mother and I would sometimes spend an afternoon looking at my baby pictures. I loved hearing her reminisce about my first steps, first words, birthdays, and other special times. Always she would recall her trip to Nova Scotia and the first time she saw and held me, and I would hear again the story of my adoption. One day, among the photos I saw a Canadian passport. Inside was a photo of an infant and two different names; one I knew as mine, and the other I wasn't sure of. When I asked my mother who the other name belonged to, she said that it was the name that my birth mother had given me when I was born. I didn't realize at the time what an important bit of information that was.

As an adult, married with children of my own, I still wondered from time to time about my birth mother. Once, on a family vacation to Nova Scotia, I made a feeble attempt to obtain a birth certificate issued in my birth name. It quickly became clear that the records had been sealed and any information about my birth parents would not be made available to me.

I don't know what prompted me to begin to search again. In February 1997, after my husband and I were on the Internet for the first time, I found the address for Parent Finders of Nova Scotia. Bob Hartlen, who was coordinating information about the Survivors of the Ideal Maternity Home, sent me information about the Home, and a whole new world opened up for me. I felt that even if I didn't find my birth family, I had found a family of Survivors, and I was one of them!

I added my name to the list of Survivors searching for birth parents and kept in touch with Bob via e-mail. Prior to my name being added to the search list, someone searching for a sibling who had been born at the Home had already registered a query. There was very little information listed. She was searching for a baby girl named Marilyn, born between 1944 and 1946.

Not long after I registered with the group, a brother to the woman who had posted the query for "Baby Girl, 1944–1946" also became involved with the group. He was able to provide a bit more information about the missing sibling. He had heard while growing up that a well-to-do Jewish couple from New Jersey had adopted her. In addition to this information, he also listed several names the baby could have been registered under at birth. This information arrived in time to be included in the next copy of the newsletter, which was sent out to all members of the group.

When I received my copy of the newsletter and noticed the update to the entry about the "Baby Girl," I was drawn to the names listed as the possible names of the birth mother. One of those names was the same as the one that was on my passport when I entered the United States as an infant. I did not act on this immediately, but with my husband urging me to follow up on it, I asked Bob if he thought there was a possibility that there could be any relationship between me and this adoptee in the newsletter.

Only days before receiving my letter, Bob had received another letter. This one was from the member who had updated the information of "Baby Girl, 1944–1946." He had noticed my new listing for "Marilyn" and found it very interesting. Recognizing that the mother's name was the same as his, and that the time frame was right, he wanted to know what the next step would be in locating his sister. This man thought that he might be my older brother, and wanted to contact me.

We spoke to each other the following morning. My mind was racing. Was this the older brother that I had wished for as a child? Did I come into the world with the knowledge that he existed? We had so many questions for each other and agreed to exchange family photographs. He also told me that he had a half-brother, and a half-sister, and

Marilyn

that it was actually the half-sister who had initiated the search for their "lost sister." I was elated but still incredulous that it could all happen with such ease and in such a short space of time.

After what seemed like an eternity, the photos arrived, and he and I spoke again. We agreed that there was nothing conclusive in the photographs, but there were some interesting resemblances among different family members. We felt that we still needed something more, something definite.

Since my adoptive mother was still living, and well, at the age of eighty-seven, I considered asking her about any papers she might have. I hesitated, however, as although she was very open about the fact that I was adopted, I felt there was still some information she did not want me to have. Hoping to avoid this confrontation, I decided to apply for a copy of my birth certificate in my birth name, also listing my birth mother's name. A letter came back stating that "based on the information contained in your request, we were unable to locate a birth registration." There was only one possibility left: to tell my adoptive mother about my possible brother and ask her if she could help us. While we were deciding what to do next, Bob received an anonymous letter postmarked from the community where my possible birth family had lived. The unsigned letter indicated that the writer was acquainted with the parties involved, and referred to the listing from the newsletter or webpage concerning a baby girl born to a person with the same name as my birth mother. The writer indicated that the father was deceased, but had a son living in Nova Scotia. Bob shared this information with us, and it became another piece of the puzzle.

I sent my mother a copy of the story of the Ideal Maternity Home. She was amazed to read about any wrongdoing at the Home. She said that everything seemed extremely well run when she was there and there was no doubt in her mind that when we left Canada I was legally hers. I asked her if she had any information about my birth parents and she told me the same story that I had heard as a child, only this time she said they had told her there was another child at home—a little boy about four years old! I then told her about the man I had been communicating with, and asked her if she had any papers with my birth mother's name on them. "Let's have a look," she said. And there it was, the Decree for Adoption and Change of Name, clearly stating that I was born on the tenth day of June, 1945, at East Chester in the County of Lunenburg, Province of Nova Scotia, giving both my birth name and that of my birth mother. What I felt in that moment cannot be put into words.

My adoptive mother was wonderful about all of it. We shared some of the photographs, and she was so happy for me, and relieved that she didn't have to keep any secrets any more. I felt that it was one of the most caring and intimate times that we had ever spent together. I telephoned my "brother" to give him the news and we spoke for a long time, neither one of us wanting to hang up. All that was needed now was to finally be able to meet for the first time and to begin catching up on all the lost years. I am eternally grateful to both of my siblings for searching for me. The fact that we were all looking for each other at the same time, and the forces that brought us together, are beyond anything that I could have imagined when I began this journey.

After making contact with the Survivors and Friends of the Ideal Maternity Home, I knew that I would be travelling to Nova Scotia in

August to attend the planned memorial service and monument dedication. Now that I had found my family, the trip would serve a two-fold purpose, the main one being to finally meet the brother that I had dreamed of for so many years. I was not only going to meet my brother; I would be meeting all three of my siblings, as well as many other relatives—aunts, uncles, cousins, nieces, and nephews.

When we finally arrived in Nova Scotia, and the weeks and months of anticipation became reality, it was everything and more than we could have expected. I not only found my family, but my heritage. Touring the province, I was introduced to the people and places that were my history. When the weekend finally arrived for the memorial, we, as a family, attended and participated. In honour of our reunion, we were invited to give the message of hope at the memorial service.

Later on, I introduced my brother to my adoptive mother. Mom told us the story of being at the Ideal Maternity Home several days after choosing me, and of waiting for the paperwork to be completed. On this particular day, there was a woman with a suitcase waiting to leave. She approached mom and the nurse, and asked if she could see her baby one last time. The nurse looked at mom and she nodded her approval. They all went to the nursery, where I was sleeping, and stood looking at me. When the nurse offered to pick me up, my birth mother said, "No, don't disturb her, she's sleeping. I just wanted to see her this one last time," and she left.

My brother and I feel very strongly that we could not have had such a meaningful reunion without the support of our loved ones—our spouses in particular—and that their continuing support is essential to the reunion process. Together, we are creating one family, discovering things about ourselves, and looking forward to the journey ahead.

The Search for Family Ties

A lice was curious, as any adopted child would be, to know what her biological parents were like. However, it wasn't until she was nineteen that she asked her adopted mother, Lillian, what her real mother looked like. Bewildered by her daughter's question, Lillian replied rather apprehensively, "She looked like me." After that, Alice kept her questions inside. Her natural curiosity was suppressed by her adopted mother's discomfort. She understood this was a painful subject for Lillian.

Alice had been raised an only child by an American Jewish couple. She knew about her adoption as far back as she could remember. Alice was told that her real mother had died in childbirth and that her real father had died in the war, leaving her an orphan. "She said my mother looked like her? How could she have seen my real mother if she had died in childbirth?" Besides, it was obvious that Lillian and Alice had nothing in common. Alice was a tall, fair-skinned, blue-eyed blonde, whereas Lillian was shorter, dark-haired, with an olive complexion.

The new story contradicted the old one. "Lillian finally told me that my mother was seventeen and unwed and there was no father in the picture. My mother had to give me up because she could not afford to raise me. With this new information, I realized that my real mother may still be alive somewhere." At that point, the search for truth began.

Alice with Lillian, Bradley Beach, NJ (summer of 1945).

Alice attending a party (the blond child in the front).

With only a birth certificate from Nova Scotia and her adopted name, Alice started gathering data on adoptions from newspapers, television programs, magazine articles, etc. "My parents seldom went out, but when they did, I searched the house frantically, trying to find my adoption papers," Alice revealed. However, nothing was ever found connecting Alice to her Canadian background.

Alice sent the number on her birth certificate to numerous sources hoping it would lead to further information.

One of the letters she received in reply told her about the Ideal Maternity Home in East Chester, Nova Scotia; a later letter confirmed that the Home had been destroyed by a fire.

With many dead ends, Alice decided to join ALMA, the Adoptees Liberty Movement Association. "I sent for an application, hoping that my mother would do the same, and that there'd be a match." But ALMA did not respond to her inquiries about Canadian adoptions. She then wrote to Parent Finders, who confirmed the existence of the Ideal Maternity Home and linked it to black market adoption to the United States.

When Alice's adopted father, Albert, passed away in January 1983, she finally found her adoption papers. "As I was looking in the safety deposit box for the burial plot insurance policy, I saw my adoption papers lying in the box. I cried because I was holding the same papers that my real mother once held. This was the nearest I had ever been to her since I was born. I learned that I was Constance Elaine MacLeod, illegitimate baby girl of Elva Gladys MacLeod from Bathurst, New Brunswick, Canada. I couldn't believe I now knew my mother's name!"

Alice sent letters to agencies in New Brunswick and found there was only one MacLeod in the Bathurst phone book—it belonged to Evan MacLeod. Alice planned to call the number whenever she was able to visit Bathurst.

In March 1992, after "The Oprah Winfrey Show" aired a reunion of people who were separated for one reason or another from their parents, Alice wrote to Evan MacLeod, asking if he had any information about Elva Gladys MacLeod. He didn't reply, but a woman, named Effie, did. She claimed to be a good friend of Elva's (that's why Evan had given her the letter) and offered information.

Alice learned that her birth mother was a married twenty-year-old, who was three or four months pregnant when her husband told her that he was leaving her for another woman. Elva went to the Ideal Maternity Home in East Chester, Nova Scotia, to have her baby on May 12, 1945. For two weeks they brought her baby to her, and then one morning told her that Constance Elaine had died the previous night. Elva became hysterical and they sedated her. She was not shown a body, only a freshly dug grave. "I was taken from her to be sold to a couple from the United States who couldn't have children. This was my black market adoption. Being a mother now, I can't bear the thought of losing a child. My mother had to be a strong person to recover from such trauma."

Elva's baby went to Newark, New Jersey, with Lillian and Albert, ages thirty-seven and forty-two. Until she was ten, she shared a corner of her adopted parents' bedroom in a small apartment.

"The years growing up were good, mainly due to the relationship I had with my father. It was a close and loving one. He was my brother and sister and play pal all in one. I adored him, and there was no one as good and kind as he was to me."

Her relationship with her mother, however, was volatile: "Once I entered junior high, my mother and I clashed; in fact, Lillian insisted that I date only Jewish boys."

"Lillian's reaction when I told her I was marrying my husband, Randy, was not surprising. Randy was of German descent, which sent her into a fury because of the Nazis' extermination of six million Jews, as if he were responsible for it." Her father, Albert, was more liberal, since there had been several inter-faith marriages on his side of the family.

Alice moved in with an aunt to get away from Lillian's meddling. Neither of her parents attended her wedding. (Not long after, Alice and Randy had a second wedding ceremony in the West Orange City Hall attended by Lillian and Albert. There was a small gathering of relatives for a gift-giving celebration. Albert and Lillian were very generous.)

Through their frequent letters, Effie and Alice developed a friendship. After returning from a trip to Nova Scotia to check out some information, Effie informed Alice that her mother had died in 1984 or 1985. "I had already accepted it once, for the first nineteen years of my life, that my mother was dead, so this wasn't hard for me to deal with."

But it was puzzling. Effie claimed to be "as one with Elva," yet she couldn't give the exact date or even year that Alice's mother had died. This led Alice to believe that Effie was her real mother, because Effie knew things that only her mother could know—like about her mother's difficult labour and how sick she was when she discovered that her daughter had been given away.

Alice continued to correspond in writing with Effie, and phone calls soon followed. On September 15, 1992, Effie called Alice. In a rather shaky but serious tone, she revealed, "I am your mother, darling. I am Elva Gladys MacLeod."

Alice's mother explained that when she went to Nova Scotia, she found proof that Alice was indeed the baby that she gave birth to. Because of all the mixing up of babies that was going on at the maternity home, Effie didn't want to say anything before she knew for sure.

Alice learned that she had an older brother and sister, nieces, nephews, and even twin grandnieces. Alice went to Bathurst to meet her mother that same fall. "We fell into one another's arms. I had a big, hollow feeling; like a balloon releasing air. It was a feeling of relief because I finally had my arms around the person who gave me life. My mother turned out to be a spunky, 5'4" lady with a pitiful pug nose like mine. I realized that this was the beginning of my life with my new family—one that would continue forever!

$\mathcal{D}$elighted to $\mathcal{B}$e $\mathcal{F}$ound

$$\boxed{\textbf{G A I L}}$$

$\mathcal{I}$ was born at the Ideal Maternity Home in secrecy. Little did my adoptive parents know when they chose me and took me to my new home in the Unites States, that the adoption would be part of a controversy in later months. On June 19, 1946, William and Lila Young were convicted of unlawfully giving out for adoption a child (me) under the age of three, kept or maintained in a Maternity Boarding House, without the consent of the Children's Aid Society. This was contrary to the new 1940 Maternity Boarding House Act of Nova Scotia. As a result, they were found guilty, and on June 29, 1946, they were ordered to pay a fine of $100.

I was born on November 4, 1945, and was adopted when I was only a few months old by an older Jewish couple from Pittsburgh, Pennsylvania. My adoptive mother was thirty-eight years old and my father forty-two. This meant that they were too old to be considered by most adoption agencies in the United States.

My adoptive parents reluctantly decided to adopt, after eighteen years of trying to have children of their own. My dad wasn't thrilled about the idea of adoption. I think he went along with it because my mother was so desperate to have a child.

I had always known that I was adopted and that my parents made me feel "special." My mother told me, "You were the most beautiful baby there." Much later I saw my passport picture. I was scrawny, bald as a cue ball, and in general, not the most beautiful baby anywhere. I was

L-R Gail at 4 months,
and 4 years old.

Gail and her adoptive father.

Gail

Gail with her husband, Jim,
son, Jason, and daughter, Jodi.

bald until I was two years old. Mother used to scotch tape a pink ribbon to my head so people would know I was a girl.

My aunt went with my mother to Nova Scotia to get me. I was not in good shape. I had rickets, some kind of skin condition, and was very scrawny. Mother had a revelation that God wanted her to take this baby and help her. I was in a hospital for almost a week before I was well enough to travel.

Dad's doubts about the idea of adoption lasted only until the plane landed. He said something like, "Here's my beautiful daughter," and remained gaga over me for the rest of his life.

Both of my adoptive parents are gone now. Mother died in 1985, and dad in 1992. I've been married to my husband, Jim, for twenty years.

On January 26, 1998, my half-brother, who lives in Nova Scotia, visited the website "Butterbox Babies" on the Internet, in search of his long-lost sister. His mother had told him of my birth and adoption.

With the assistance of several resourceful people within the adoption community, via the Internet, I was located. On February 12, Bob sent me information concerning my birth family and their search for me. While at the time I was not actively searching, I was delighted to be found.

A couple of days later, I heard from my brother. He assured me he didn't want to push himself into my life. I replied, "I have plenty of room in my life for new people; let's get to know each other." Soon after that, I received a letter from my birth mother. It was difficult to know how to respond to her letter, let alone enter into a new relationship with her.

I have never felt any special need to search out my birth parents. I truly felt that I had all the family anyone could want or need. After fifty-two years of thinking that I would never know about my origins, it is stunning to find out that my birth mother is alive and that I have brothers and a sister. I am very glad that we have found each other.

It occurs to me after reading all the horrifying details of what went on at the Home that I probably wasn't far from a butterbox myself. If my adoptive mother had chosen a beautiful, healthy child, I probably wouldn't be here. That is a very scary thought.

See Mary's story, "I Can Die in Peace," on page 17.

"Don't Tell Ilene"

$\mathcal{I}$ was adopted from the Ideal Maternity Home in East Chester, Nova Scotia, in the summer of 1945, by a Jewish couple in their thirties who could not have a child of their own. Tessie Kaplan and Bernie Seifer had been married for eleven years before they found a child to adopt. Tessie's parents were first cousins from Russia. She was a hypochondriac and suffered from undiagnosed bi-polar disorder. Bernie was the youngest child of Polish immigrants and learned the paper-hanging trade from his father-in-law, who owned a successful paint business in Newark, NJ.

Bernie adored me, but Tessie's illnesses overshadowed our family, preventing a warm loving atmosphere. Besides feeling different, I also didn't look at all like my parents. I was fair-haired with a turned-up nose. People always remarked about my looks being so unlike theirs. I remember staring in the mirror in later years wondering, "Who am I and where did I come from?"

I recall being taunted in the schoolyard when I was about seven years old. "Ha ha, you're adopted, ha ha, you're adopted," a little girl kept chanting at me. I ran home and told my mother about what had happened. She didn't say it wasn't true. I had an awful feeling in my chest and stomach.

My parents told me I was born while they were on vacation in Canada. This always seemed strange because my parents never travelled. I knew vaguely from overhearing hushed conversations that there were a lot of other children from Canada in my school. Their names were whispered. My parents suddenly had new friends. They were older couples with only one child, like in our family. Those children also looked out of place with their parents. The undercurrent of secrecy was part of my parents' life.

Every summer on television there were warnings for resident aliens to renew their green cards or be subject to deportation. I was always afraid I would be deported because I didn't have a green card. I never told anyone. I was also terrified when I found out women were drafted in Israel. Because my parents were Jewish, I thought I would be drafted into the Israeli army. I was seven years old and afraid. My parents went to their graves without telling me I was adopted.

At my insistence, I was naturalized a month before my eighteenth birthday. I was fearful that I would no longer be a minor and could get into trouble with Immigration. My application papers were stamped "Confidential." I was asked only one question: "Who was the first president of the United States?"

I was sworn in as a citizen in a courtroom full of people. I felt strange being there with the majority of new citizens barely speaking English. The night I became a citizen, I saw the papers I had been trying to find over the years. I had borrowed my father's car, and they were locked in the glove compartment. I read them and saw my birth mother's name, which was then branded in my memory. Over thirty years would pass before I would contact her.

Today, I know that aside from love, one of the reasons I married my first husband was because of his happy, loving home and family. His parents had three sons. I became the daughter they always wanted. I loved being at their house. I was always searching for a mother, and my mother-in-law filled that role beautifully. I still talk to her almost every day, even though her son and I have been apart for fifteen years. In contrast, the day before my wedding, I had to pick up my mother Tessie from the psychiatric ward, where she had been receiving shock treatments.

My father and I made all the wedding arrangements together. Tessie was incapable of giving me the basics. I never felt close to her.

When my first son, Adam Rossi, was born two years later, I was thrilled to finally have someone who was a part of me—my own flesh and blood. I was hurt when my relatives said repeatedly how much he looked like them. No one else can know what it's like for an adopted person when their first child is born.

Ilene

Ilene and husband, Steve (1998).

Ilene with sons Adam (white shirt) and Justin (black shirt).

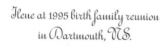

Ilene at 1995 birth family reunion in Dartmouth, NS.

My second son, Justin, was born four years later. After my sons were born, I would occasionally think that one day I would find "her." I would imagine she always longed for me on my birthday, and was wondering what happened to me. How wrong I was.

I began my quest for my birth family in 1995, after both my adoptive parents were dead. My second husband, Steve, began to help me search by contacting the Immigration and Naturalization Service for papers from my naturalization. Several months later, we received a copy of my original birth certificate, Canadian adoption papers, a visa to enter the U.S., and other documents relating to my adoption. There was her name again. With this information, we set out to find her.

A simple phone call to information in Halifax connected me to my first cousin Janice who lives in Dartmouth. She said my mother was alive, but probably wouldn't want to have anything to do with me. My mother had married a man (not my father) that she met during her pregnancy. They never had any children, and her husband had died a few years ago. She told me I was from the Ideal Maternity Home and a Butterbox Baby Survivor. My mother's family was from Newfoundland; they lived on an island that is now uninhabited.

I was terribly disappointed that my mother wasn't searching for me. I kept thinking that maybe Janice was wrong. Maybe my mother never revealed the deepest parts of her heart to anyone.

Janice and I agreed to exchange photos. When the photos arrived, there was a picture of my mother in her early teens. I had a photograph of myself at the same age—we could have been twins!

Through another cousin, I found out I was born in Halifax at the Grace Maternity Hospital, and taken to the Ideal Maternity Home five days later. My mother cried the whole way there, and sobbed the whole way back. After that day she never spoke of me again. I found out that one of my earlier attempts to find my mother had almost paid off. An investigator had made contact with a cousin, who got in touch with my mother and her husband. My stepfather wanted to get on a plane and come to New Jersey immediately, but another cousin who was an adoptive parent dissuaded them. That cousin feared a biological parent coming between him and his child, and projected those feelings into my situation. It was enough to prevent the reunion, and delay my knowing about my birth family for several years.

My cousins were reluctant to tell my mother I wanted to contact her, so I wrote and sent photos. A reply came a month later. Unfortunately for me, she felt it was better to leave things in the past. She said my adoptive parents were my parents, and she didn't want me to contact her again. Now I knew for certain, the worst was true. She didn't want me.

Janice had sent me the book *Butterbox Babies*. Reading it helped me to understand what a horrible stigma had been placed on unwed mothers in that era. One passage tells of a health inspector's visit to the Home in the middle of summer. There were eighty babies in a large room with closed windows. They were all crying and there were a great number of flies on the infants. One woman was taking care of all of them. I realized from the date of the report that I was one of those babies. Before I knew about where I came from, I had always felt I was never held as an infant. It seems I was right. The stress of finally finding my mother, being rejected, and then discovering the incredible story of the Ideal Maternity Home was enormous.

I felt that I had to speak to someone else who shared my background. I called Bette Cahill, and was put in touch with Michael Reider. He referred me to a woman named Sandy, who also lived in New Jersey. She was happy to help me through my emotional turmoil. Sandy was in touch with another Survivor, Alice, whom I knew from grammar school. Alice had been told that she was adopted, but had been cautioned by her parents, "Don't tell Ilene!"

Sandy, Alice, and I met for lunch. We talked for hours. The similarities in our lives were amazing. We were all only children, raised by Jewish parents, and had all felt uncomfortable growing up, as if we didn't fit in with our families. Discovering they had the same feelings validated how I had felt.

With Sandy's encouragement I went to Nova Scotia. I cried during the whole flight. All the years of wondering about my family, and now I was finally going to meet them face to face.

My cousins Janice and Don met me at the airport. I hugged them and couldn't stop staring at them. We sat outside my mother's apartment building and I looked up at her window. I still hoped for a chance meeting. I saw where I was born, and the school and church I would have attended. I was dazed by all my eyes took in. I loved Nova Scotia as soon as I got there. Its beauty, history, and pace impressed me deeply. I felt so comfortable and serene with my surroundings. It was like home. Sandy was right. I needed to see it, smell the air, and feel it.

It was wonderful to meet my aunts. I felt such love from them. Another cousin had a barbecue and all my relatives—except my mother—came to be with me. I was the long-lost child of their family.

I keep in touch with my Canadian family through letters, phone calls, and e-mail. I have visited every summer since we made contact. My husband called my mother after our visit for the 1997 memorial ceremony to get information about my biological father. She had seen me on television, unveiling the monument, but still wouldn't speak to me. That Christmas, I mailed her a pair of gloves and a Christmas card. She returned them both.

Revealing the secret surrounding my birth has set me free. I no longer feel any shame. I have answers to the questions about my past, new relatives, and very importantly, a medical history. I feel so grateful to have survived, and blessed to have found new love from my biological family and from other Survivors.

"A Chosen Child"

SUSAN

It was a dismal, snowy day in November 1945 when my adoptive parents started their long journey to the Ideal Maternity Home. They travelled from New Jersey to Boston, in spite of severe weather conditions, then boarded a train for New Brunswick. There they met with a lawyer named Benjamin Guss, who was working with Dr. and Mrs. Young. He advised my parents go to East Chester, and meet the Youngs in person. When they arrived at their destination, the conductor stopped the train in a snow-covered field and pointed to a house that had a large sign on the roof indicating that they had babies for sale.

On meeting the Youngs, my parents told them they wanted a baby girl. Lila took them to the nursery, where they fell in love with a dark-haired, green-eyed baby—me. They also met my birth mother, who was working off her debt to the Youngs. It must have been heart-wrenching for her to give me up, but she was young, unmarried, and barely able to keep herself alive. She loved me and took care of me in the nursery, especially at night. She would rock me to sleep, knowing in her heart that she wanted me to have a better life than what she could offer me at that time.

After my parents chose me, they completed the simple adoption process, and, accompanied by the Youngs, went to town to buy the items I would need to begin my life with my new family. That night, they caught the train back to New Brunswick, accompanied by my birth mother, to meet with Benjamin Guss and legalize the adoption.

I have known that I was adopted since I was five years old. My parents had told me that I was special, because I was "a chosen child." I was told that my father had died in the war and my mother shortly after that. I didn't find out my birth name and the fact that I was Canadian until I was seventeen years old, and needed a copy of my birth certificate to obtain my driver's license.

Susan (passport photo)
—November 15, 1945.

When I was thirty-two years old, with my husband and two children in tow, I drove to Canada to begin the search for my birth family. My efforts proved futile.

In June 1997, I stumbled across a movie called *Butterbox Babies*. I sat glued to the television, fascinated as the story of my life, as well as that of many others, unfolded. I called my mother and told her to turn on the television. The story of the Youngs did not agree with my parents' personal accounts. The story portrayed them as money-hungry, scheming, and deceitful people. My parents felt they were generally concerned about the welfare of the babies living in the Home. The nursery was clean, and there was no evidence of disease when they were there.

Two weeks later, I found a newspaper article about a brother and sister who were adopted from the Ideal Maternity Home. I gathered my courage and telephoned one of them. Here I was, crying my heart out to a complete stranger. Within days I met more adoptees from the Home, and later went to a "Butterbox Baby Survivor" reunion held in Nova Scotia.

Over seventy adoptees from the Ideal Maternity Home, from all over North America, gathered in Nova Scotia on Labour Day weekend, 1987. Other than my life with my husband and the birth of our two children, the reunion invoked the single most wonderful feeling I have ever experienced. Finally, I was on the way to finding my birth family.

After the reunion, I contacted a private investigator named Jeannie McMullin from New Brunswick. Within two months, Jeannie telephoned me to say she thought she had found my birth mother. I was in shock. But when I contacted the woman who was possibly my birth mother, she said that I was not her daughter. I called Jeannie back, and she was still confident this woman was my birth mother.

Three days later, my husband and I were on our way to visit friends, and my daughter called us on the car phone and said, "Your birth mother is looking for you." I couldn't wait to get to a telephone to call her back.

After my mother had denied me when I telephoned her, she sat down with my four sisters and brother, and told them about me. They couldn't wait to meet me. My mother apologized for denying me and explained that she was in shock and just couldn't handle the news when I called.

In April 1998, my husband and I went to Canada to meet my new family. I finally felt a true sense of belonging when I met the woman who had given birth to me, fifty-two years ago. My birth mother and I share similar features, likes and dislikes, and yes, she did—and still does—love me.

I feel like a new person, with self-esteem I never had before. My only regret is that I didn't get to meet my family sooner.

Susan's birth mother and adoptive mother in front of the Court House in New Brunswick, December 1945.

THE SONS SPEAK

Our Nova Scotia Trip

J I M

My name is Jim, and I was born on April 15, 1942. My story begins in early May 1996. I received a phone call from the Adoption Services Office in Fredericton. The caller informed me that I had a birth sister who was looking for me and asked me if I would agree to let the service give her my address. I agreed, and shortly after, on May 13, I received a letter from my sister, Lillian. I drove to Boston in late June to meet her and visit for a few days. I was shocked that we looked so much alike and that we share similar mannerisms, likes and dislikes.

I found Lillian's history very interesting. She was born on March 26, 1939, in Saint John, New Brunswick, and was placed for adoption in the New Brunswick Protestant Orphans Home on April 6, 1939. As a child, she had a serious speech impediment and "crow's toes," which made her very clumsy. She also had a sensitivity to light and spent hours in the basement. These physical problems put her on the unadoptable list. As luck would have it, a woman who was adopted from the same home as a child had sworn to return some day and take some other little girl out of there. Her name was Ethel Benson. Ethel went to the home several times trying to decide which girl she should help. Lillian remembers approaching a man and woman and saying, "Daddy, Mommy take me home." Apparently, Ethel knew then that Lillian was the one. Lillian's new parents took her to the States, where her father had found work. Her parents bought her corrective shoes, and glasses, and they sent her to vocal lessons for her speech impediment. Ethel was a hard worker

who did domestic cleaning jobs and often took Lillian with her. Lillian had a happy childhood, and went on to become a nurse. Although she married, she never had any children of her own. Lillian's mother and father both died several years ago. I often think what would have happened to Lillian if she had been born in the Ideal Maternity Home. Ethel was a very special and loving woman and mother.

I was also an adopted child. After meeting Lillian, I learned that my Aunt Doris had my adoption papers. She gave them to me, along with a copy of my grandmother's poem about her and mother's trip to Chester to get me. My grandmother liked to write poetry, and did so on every trip that I can remember her taking. My Aunt Doris was in the Air Force during the war, and she remembers taking a leave for two weeks in July 1943 so that she could come home to see me. I was about fifteen months old at the time. She was told that my mother and grandmother went to Nova Scotia to adopt a girl. Apparently, while they were waiting in a large room, I crawled up on my mother's lap and grabbed her pearls and broke them, causing the beads to roll all over the floor. My grandmother said that she didn't have to choose a child as I had chosen her. She said it was the Lord's will. I must say that she certainly loved and cared for me over the years; she turned ninety the week of the 1997 reunion in Nova Scotia.

Lillian did a lot of research into our parents. It is likely that my father was born January 19, 1873, in Sunderland, England. I can't be certain, as the name Reed was often recorded as Reid, or Reidit. He was a married man who ran a grocery store on the corner of Sydney and Britain streets in Saint John. Ironically, I now own the house on the corner of Britain and Wentworth streets that he once owned, and where he lived at the time of his death on May 16, 1952. I had no knowledge of him when I bought the property of six units some twenty years ago. It was run down and my wife asked me why I would ever buy a property in such disrepair. I remember I told her it has a strange appeal to me and that I could restore it. I have done a lot of work on the place and it has changed a lot since the 1950s. I thought about selling it, but now I'm glad I didn't.

My mother was born December 16, 1922, in Saint John, one of fifteen Irish children. I believe that she worked at my father's store part time but the city directory lists her at the sugar refinery in the early 1940s. Lillian has met our mother on several occasions but has promised our aunts not to tell her that she is her birth daughter. I met her once in church and also kept my identity to myself. I was curious, but didn't want to impose on her as I believe she wants to put her teenage past behind her.

I have been divorced for fifteen years. In another twist of fate, my girlfriend lives in the same apartment in east Saint John that my birth mother moved out of several years ago. Of course, she was not aware of that when she moved in. I spend a lot of time there. Also, my birth mother lives in the same nursing home as my adoptive mother and they each have a sister living there.

We believe that we had a brother born at the Ideal Maternity Home in late 1940; apparently he was stillborn. But the records are so vague, we are not certain if he died or was sold.

In the book *Butterbox Babies*, there was mention of a Ben Guss, who was a prominent criminal lawyer in Saint John. He also arranged mortgages with prominent business men—I think that my uncle and father both dealt with him, and he may have brokered my adoption.

The following is a poem that my adoptive grandmother wrote when she and my mother went to Nova Scotia to adopt me. While it does not mention me, it does say a lot about the times, the method of travel, and the amount of time it took to get there and back. It gives the number of babies at the Home on that weekend. One can assume that the Youngs treated many of the prospective adoptive parents in a similar manner, providing them with shopping trips, tours of the area, and dinner.

> Our Nova Scotia Trip—May 19, 20, and 21, 1943
> *I went at six in the morning, to the residence of Ora Parlee.*
> *After rousing them out of bed, we soon made toast and tea.*
> *Then Marjorie and I took the Glen Falls bus, on the first lap of*
> *the way,*
> *And at Haymarket changed to the South End bus, for the boat*
> *down at the bay.*
> *We boarded the* Princess Helena, *at fifteen minutes to eight;*
> *But had to wait for service men, whose train was an hour late.*
> *At fifteen to nine we left Saint John for Digby across the bay.*
> *We remained on deck and stood by the rail, almost all of the way.*

The day was fine and the water calm, so what could we ask
    for more.
Two hours and a half from when we left Saint John, we reached
    Nova Scotia's shore.
We went right to the train at Digby, as we didn't want to be late,
And asked for dinner a board the train, but some airmen were
    dining in state.
So we had three hours or more to wait, before they let us in.
And when at last they gave us a call, the chicken I ate was a sin.
But my tea, my lovely cup of tea, I couldn't hold with a hawser;
I managed to get one nice big sup, then it flew right into the saucer.
We rocked and we rolled, and the country looked so bare.
Rocks, rocks on every side, with a green field here and there,
Like an oasis in the desert, to cheer us on our way,
And beckon, do come back again, when you can longer stay.
We saw them erecting a naval base, for a good ten thousand
    and strong.
We won't say where, but we noticed it, as the train she sped
    along.
Some of the boys were out on parade, and others just came there,
On a special train that followed us from Saint John and
    elsewhere.
We passed through Annapolis Royal, Bridgetown, and Paradise.
There were now a few more orchards, and some parts were
    really nice,
With oxen working in the fields, and grass so nice and green.
The apple trees had just been sprayed, to kill the grubs I seen.
We reached the town of Middleton, with a good half hour to stay.
So we started out a searching, to find a restaurant or cafe.
We walked for half a mile or more, for just cold drinks and candy.
I said to the store keeper, you should have a restaurant handy.
She said there was a restaurant, near the depot in the town,
But one day it caught a fire, and begorra it burnt down.
So we hurried to the depot, and again got on the train,
As we didn't want to miss it, and in that place remain.
We travelled down to Bridgewater, near the setting of the sun,

The land here looked more arable, and cropping nearly done.
Large orchards everywhere around, but we began to stare
At a hundred apple trees or more, with roots up in the air.
It must have been a heavy gale, that blew this section round,
And flung those lovely apple trees, uprooted from the ground.
The oxen here again hold sway, no horses to be seen,
And settlements with houses large, and lawns so nice and clean.
We passed by Albany and Springfield, and then New Germany,
Which is most prosperous of them at least it seemed to me.
We reached the town of Bridgewater, a little past sundown,
And gathering up our luggage, we began to look around.
Of all the hotels in this burg, the Waverley looked best,
To get a good night's lodging, at which we were now in quest.
But they had no vacant rooms, so next we tried LaHave,
Where we got a room and supper, 'bout which Marge began to
      rave.
The fried eggs were like leather, and the bacon was so small,
That if it hadn't been charged on the bill, we'd thought we had
      none at all.
As it was too early yet for bed, we wondered where we'd go.
After thinking it over for a while, we decided to take in a show.
We had breakfast at La Have again, then to Chester took the train.
It was looking very cloudy, and we thought it sure would rain.
But the fog was clearing up a bit, when we passed by Mahone Bay.
And when we got to Chester, 'twas a nice sunshiny day.
We were guests while there in Chester, of Dr. Young and wife,
And for motoring and sightseeing, we had the time of our life.
We had dinner at the Doctor's, then Mrs. Young took the car,
And out we went a shopping, to the stores near and far.
We visited The Ideal home, and looked the children over.
Fifty-three, not past years two, and them expecting more.
With a Dr. and three nurses, I guess they got good care.
But as our stay was getting short, we did not loiter there.
We stayed with the Youngs for supper, then she drove us to the
      train,
And with our visit over, we started home again.

'Twas eight o'clock in the evening, when at Bridgewater we pulled in.
We hailed ourselves a taxi, and went to the Hillside Inn.
Leaving our luggage in the room, I walked up the Main Street,
And noted where a restaurant was, at which we next would eat.
I wrote and mailed some post cards, then home and soon to bed.
Marjorie said she was so tired, that she was nearly dead.
At seven in the morning, we donned our travelling clothes,
And went for a lovely breakfast, to a tearoom named Red Rose.
We walked up to the station, took the train at fifteen to nine.
And so back again to Middleton we travelled the same old line.
At noon we left for Digby and reaching there at two,
We started for a restaurant but those air force boys in blue
Had once more beat us to it. Oh they surely got our goat.
We grabbed ourselves a taxi and went right to the boat.
We went right to the dining saloon, I said we're surely able
To have dinner here in peace, so we found ourselves a table.
A waitress gave us a menu but didn't come back for an hour,
And to attract their attention was away beyond our power.
Tables were reserved for air force men who had made reservations,
Perhaps much earlier in the day from some of the back stations.
And the waitresses all a smile were serving the boys in blue,
So just sit and wait while they dined in state, was all that we
    could do.
But the civilians got their dinner at last, after waiting an hour
    or more.
And soon they loosened all the lines and we left the Digby shore.
The sea was rough, but we wasn't sick, and stayed for a while
    below.
Then came again to the upper deck and watched a sub chaser go.
The port of Saint John, we reached at last and on the bus and
    home.
I'll take a thermos and carry a lunch if we any more do roam
While the war is on and the servicemen reserve all food en
    route.
So I'll say good bye as our trip is done, nothing more to tell you
    about.

From Adoption to Closure, with Love

BOB HARTLEN

J was born Robert Vennall on June 22, 1945, and adopted by a wonderful couple, Wilson and Maude Hartlen, of Halifax. They were the best mom and dad a kid could ever want. Our family life focused on each other; we were happy, our home was full of love, and we shared a lot of activities and quality time together. Memories of my early years are scattered, but I recall that our extended family was constantly in touch with each other. I was brought up in the city of Halifax, which, in the late 1940s, was almost like rural areas of the province today; we even kept chickens and geese during those early years. I remember my parents building our first house in a forested area, which we moved into when I was five years old.

I was born at a time of great change, following the end of World War II. Being in a new neighbourhood, there were many other children, most of us around the same age. Although I was an only child, there was always someone to play with, and I was never aware of a sense of loneliness. Our family was always doing something together. This was before television, and we spent a lot of time visiting friends and family. In the evenings, after my homework was done, we listened to the radio, or played games. My dad and I went to the movies every week, and we went out to the country to visit my great grandmother every weekend. This was usually a good time, as all of the cousins and aunts and uncles also went to visit Grandma on Sunday. The adults visited with her, and the kids played in the orchard. In fact, all special occasions were family occasions. We even went shopping together, and on grocery day our special treat was "cream soda ice-cream floats" after supper. It's nice to recall something so natural as my mom, dad, and me sitting around the kitchen table together, scooping ice cream into tumblers of cream soda. That is what my life was like—till I was nine years old.

My bedroom was beside mom and dad's, and one night I woke up to the sound of my father calling out in pain. I could hear my mother talking with him, and crying. Mom called the doctor, and awakened some of our roomers living upstairs, who came downstairs to help. I was too afraid to come out of my room to find out what was happening. Soon an ambulance arrived, and suddenly everything was quiet again, so I came out of my room. Mom and dad were gone, and the bedclothes were scattered on the floor. One of our roomers was in the living room, obviously there to look after me if I woke up. He told me not to worry, that my dad was sick and he had to go to the hospital, and that my mom had gone with him. He tried to reassure me, but I knew that something was really wrong. My dad had been sick before, but nothing like this. Mom came home an hour or so later. I knew then that something had happened. One of the women who also lived in our house was with her, and they were both crying. My dad had died of a cerebral hemorrhage.

Over the next few days, my mom was either at the funeral home, or just sitting and crying at home. I couldn't believe that my dad was gone. He seemed all right that day—we read the comics in the evening like we always did—I just couldn't believe it.

The evening before the funeral, I went with mom to the funeral home. When I saw my dad lying there in his coffin, reality hit me. For the first time since I had been told that he died, I started to cry. I knew now that he was really gone. I remember not wanting to leave him there that night, and finally going home and my mother sitting with me until I eventually cried myself to sleep. The day of the funeral, I was too hysterical to go, and stayed at home with one of the women who lived in our house.

Life as I had known it changed drastically. My mom was now a widow and a single mother, with a nine-year-old child and two homes to care

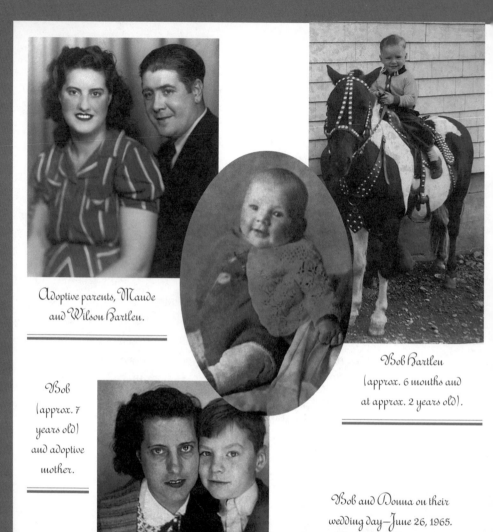

Adoptive parents, Maude
and Wilson Hartlen.

Bob Hartlen
(approx. 6 months and
at approx. 2 years old).

Bob
(approx. 7
years old)
and adoptive
mother.

Bob and Donna on their
wedding day—June 26, 1965.

Bob
(19 years old).

for by herself. She and dad had purchased the home we were living in a few months before his death. Unfortunately, both being young and healthy, they didn't take advantage of the optional mortgage insurance, leaving her with a mortgage to look after as well. She had to go to work full time. Fortunately, we did have the roomers upstairs, but even though this was additional income, it was also more work for her.

One evening, shortly after my father died, my mom called me into the kitchen and told me that there was something she had to tell me. After reassuring me that she loved me, she told me that I had been adopted when I was a baby, and showed me the adoption papers. The news had little impact on me; she and dad had been the only parents that I had ever known, and as far as I was concerned she was my mother. The adoption papers didn't mean anything to me either, but I did remember my birth mother's name—Violet Vennall. After telling me I was adopted, she put the papers in the stove, saying that we didn't need them anymore. Little did she realize that the day would come when I would desperately need them. I believe she felt she was doing the right thing; those papers were a reminder that someone else had given birth to me. Just the thought of another woman saying she was my mother was a threat to her. When, as an adult, I found my birth mother, mom was extremely intimidated and afraid that I would forget all about her. That fear was there till the day I told mom of my birth mother's death.

Gradually, we adjusted to life without dad, but with mom working full time I was often alone. When I came home from school, instead of being able to play with the other kids, I had chores to do, such as preparing the vegetables for supper, and cleaning up my room. I could play after supper for a while, but had to be in at a reasonable time to do my homework and go to bed early so I could get up for school in the morning. There were no more family games or going to the movies in the evenings anymore. Eventually, mom made arrangements for me to board with a family with children through the week, so that I wouldn't be alone so much, and would be supervised while she was working. She had to be out to work by five o'clock in the morning, and she felt that I was too young to get myself off to school. I came home on weekends, but neither of us was happy being separated through the week. It was during these years that I started to think about my "real family." I would fantasize that I had lots of brothers and sisters and that my real family had just made a mistake. I could imagine my "real" mother living in a big house and trying to find me. Although as a teenager I was very curious about my "real family," I had no idea how to find them. I remember going to the library and trying to find the name Vennall in the books of surnames, but found nothing that gave me any clues.

When I finished school, I went to community college. The most eventful thing that happened there was that I met Donna, the girl that I fell in love with and eventually married. I later left school and home and joined the army to gain some independence. Donna and I, both seventeen and madly in love, decided that we wanted to get married. Our families wouldn't hear of it (in those days you needed parental permission if underage) so the wedding bells didn't ring for a couple of years.

In the meantime, my mom dated a bit and established a social life for herself. But she was still mom, waiting and hoping that I would someday move back home. I did, but only for a few months until Donna and I were married. Just four days after my twentieth birthday, Donna and I began our married life together. Even though I was still too young to benefit from my dad's estate, Donna and I moved into one of our houses and set up housekeeping; my mom moved into the other. Our daughter, Dawn, was born during our first year of marriage, and my mom finally accepted a proposal of marriage. She felt that she could get on with her life, now that mine was settled.

Unfortunately, her new husband, who had a drinking problem that she didn't know about, starting drinking again within a year. What should have been a relationship full of love, companionship, and happiness turned out to be the opposite. This was especially hard for her, after having had such a loving first marriage. Despite her unhappiness, she stayed in the marriage for over twenty years, rather than living alone, until her death. I think that sometimes her only salvation was that she had us, and then her grandchildren, to love and indulge.

Like a lot of young people at the time, we were concerned about raising a child in the city, so in 1967, when Dawn was a year old, I accepted a new job and we moved to Kentville, a beautiful Valley town.

After I was married, I again thought about trying to find out more about my family. In 1968, I contacted the Department of Social Services, explaining what I knew of my birth situation, and provided my mother's name, which I still remembered. I was pretty naive, thinking it would take only a telephone call to get the information that I wanted. The response was the same as many others before me had received: "We're sorry that we cannot provide any identifying information." By the time I thought of contacting the Ideal Maternity Home, I was told that the Home, and all its records, had burned. I traced one of the Youngs' children, hoping that they might have their parents' records, but they didn't. I found it hard to believe that even if my personal information was at Community Services, I wasn't entitled to it. I was a bit more anxious this time, having two children of my own, and feeling that it was important to them as well. Our son, Robert, was born in June 1968.

Several years later, my daughter became ill, and I needed medical history. She had severe headaches, accompanied by nausea and vomiting, and finally partial paralysis. This was serious, and I didn't have any medical information that could offer any clues to her illness. Dawn had test after test, with no conclusive evidence what the problem was or how to treat it. Exploratory surgery was suggested, which I couldn't subject my daughter to, so long as there was any alternative.

I contacted the Department of Social Services several times, begging for information. If ever a person needs an occasion to humble themselves, this is the ideal way to do it. Failing to elicit their help or compassion, I tried to find other families with the Vennall name. I also contacted Parent Finders to begin a search with their help. I spent time at the Maritime phone company, looking through directories from the east to west coast. There was one Vennall family in the Halifax directory, and I used the excuse of genealogy to make an inquiry, but they didn't have any information that could help. Years later, after I had found my mother and met my sisters, I learned that the Vennall in Halifax was my birth mother's brother-in-law. I often wonder if he would have given me the information I needed if I had been more direct in my inquiry.

In the interim, I continued to phone the Department of Community Services to beg for information. This time I must have tweaked a heart string somewhere, because I received a clue that I needed. They told me that my mother used "Mrs" before her name and that she had listed Cobourg, Ontario, as her place of residence. I searched through the

Ontario directories, found the town of Cobourg, and there among the V's was a "V. Vennall." I wrote at once, explaining the circumstances of my birth, my search for my natural parents, and my need for medical information. I did not involve my family at this stage; if I was to receive rejection I wanted to deal with it alone. Within a week, I received a letter from Violet Vennall, telling me that I had found the person I had been looking for. She was my mother. She pleaded with me not to communicate with any of "her" family, and said she would deny everything and I would never hear from her again. She told that I had five sisters. The eldest was the daughter of her first husband, who was killed overseas, and the other four were by her present husband. She provided me with the medical background that I required. My daughter had inherited a severe type of migraine—my mother had suffered the same symptoms at a very young age. Thankfully, we could rule out exploratory surgery. With this information, our doctor prescribed several different types of medication over time, and finally brought our daughter's illness under control. Now, almost twenty years later, she rarely has migraine problems. I often shudder at what the outcome could have been had I not been able to find my birth mother and obtained the medical history. I also think of the possibly thousands of other adoptees who are dealing with similar situations with their children, and grandchildren, because they cannot access their medical histories. It is a cruel social system that allows this to happen.

Once the contact was made with Violet, I had to decide how was I going to tell my mom. I knew I had to tell her, regardless of how she would feel about it. If she found out from someone else it would really hurt her. As I told the story of finding Violet, I watched the huge tears building up in her eyes and running down her cheeks. Just knowing that she was hurting also hurt me very much. I assured her that it took more than the act of birth to make a mother, and that she was the only "real mother" I would ever have. She was the one who brought me home, loved and cared for me all these years. She was my mother and could never be replaced.

I had no doubt by the time I left that she knew how special and how loved she was. I also knew how threatened and intimidated she felt now that I had found Violet. Unfortunately I couldn't change that. In the years that followed, when we were alone, she would sometimes ask me if I ever heard from "that woman," but we never really talked about her. But I always knew who she was referring to. She only felt secure in her role as my mother after Violet died.

My birth mother and I maintained an active correspondence for the next several years until her death. She told me that she would tell me who my father was, but it was almost four years before she finally did. It was as though she was withholding the information as her insurance that I wouldn't betray her secret. Sometimes I wondered if it was worth the anguish. She was never able to see my side of things. There was a bond between us but there was no relationship; I had no desire to actually meet her in person. Although she mentioned me coming to Ontario, and of being welcome, there was still too much secrecy surrounding my birth, and too much inconsistency in her letters, regarding her feelings. I looked forward to hearing from her, but I never knew what to expect when I got a letter. Sometimes she would be so nice and thoughtful, even loving, and sometimes bitter and resentful. But even this kind of contact was better than none at all. It was pretty clear that the shame of my birth was not forgotten, or forgiven, by her husband. She didn't feel secure enough in her family to tell them about me, or to let me back into her life.

She and my birth father had been dating for several years. She was a widow, with a young child, and my dad was separated from his wife, pending divorce. When she decided to leave my birth father and marry her present husband, he knew that she was pregnant, but he married her anyway. Her husband was in the navy and stationed in Halifax. That is probably how she ended going to the Ideal Maternity Home. Its existence was well known among the servicemen, and more than one young woman went there to be rid of her "mistake."

I kept my promise not to contact my sisters, but as luck would have it, one them, Penny, was visiting my mother in Ontario when my letter arrived. Sensing something was wrong, she copied my return address. My sisters Penny and Debbie had suspected since they were young that they had a brother somewhere. They told me of overhearing arguments between their parents about "the baby," referred to as "he." As soon as she returned to her home in New Brunswick, Penny contacted me, and, after sounding me out, introduced herself as my sister. It felt strange to finally be talking with someone who was actually part of me. The following week, she and her family came to visit, and for the first time, other than my own children, I met my first blood relative.

Our visit went extremely well. It is hard to describe the feelings and emotions of that first meeting with my sister. It was as if we had known each other all of our lives. It was uncanny to discover the similarities that we shared. We definitely were family. Originally the visit was to be a short one, but fate often intervenes, especially when you are trying to keep secrets. Donna and I had decided not to mention this visit to mom or any of our family. We thought that we would be able to find the right time and circumstances to tell them and decided to keep the visit a secret. But not all secrets are meant to be kept. Donna's sister Barb had decided to pay us a surprise visit, and when she drove into the yard, her car accidentally brushed against Penny's youngest child, Junior. We all panicked. Junior was crying, Barb was beside herself, afraid she had hurt the child, and we were so concerned that although we were sure Junior was all right, we took him to outpatients anyway. We didn't think about introductions. After the introductions were finally made, Barb felt even worse, thinking that she had interrupted our reunion under these circumstances. The doctor recommended that Junior remain in hospital overnight just as a precaution, so Peggy's visit was extended. Our secret remained a secret from the rest of the family until we had chance to tell everyone in person. Penny and I maintained a close relationship for several years, but eventually the letters got further and further apart and finally stopped for a while. Fortunately, they have resumed and we are in contact again.

I eventually contacted all of my sisters after my mother's death and met them in person several years later. Of my five sisters, I have a relationship with three of them: Penny, Pat, and Fran. They all live in Ontario, and visits are few and far between, but we have bonded as brother and sister, and although we don't see each other often, they are a very important part of my life. My other two sisters have chosen not to pursue our relationship, and I have to respect that decision, although that doesn't make them any less my sisters, and they are often in my thoughts. Recently, while Penny was visiting them in Ontario, they all had their picture taken together, and I was sent a copy.

In 1990, I decided that if I was ever going to find my father while there was a chance that he was still living, I had better get started. My mother had told me my father's name before she died. His name wasn't common to the east coast, and I thought there was a good chance that he too was from Ontario, possibly from the Cobourg or surrounding areas. With my mother gone, I didn't feel bound by my promise not to search for him. Finding him couldn't hurt her anymore. Again, I had to consider the outcome. If I was successful in finding him, would my father accept me or reject me? After my relationship with my mother, I had to give that serious thought. I decided to keep an open mind and be prepared to accept the outcome, whatever it was. I couldn't really be sure that the name my mother gave me was the right one, as many of the things she told me had proven to be contradictory. At any rate, I was prepared to search for Arthur Fulford, the name she gave me.

I searched for the Fulford name in the communities close to Cobourg. I found several Fulfords and sent out letters requesting genealogical information about the Fulford family, and particularly about Arthur Fulford. Within a short time, I received a reply to one of my letters, signed by Art Fulford, requesting information about my connection with the family, my mother, and my birth information. I felt I had nothing to lose and sent all of the information that I had. It was only after I met my dad that I found out he had always suspected that he had a child by Violet, but was never able to confirm or find any proof of it, and finally, after many years, gave up the search.

About a week after answering Art Fulford's letter, someone called asking to speak with my wife. She was not home so he asked me if she had written to Art Fulford, looking for information. My mouth went dry and I told him that I, not my wife, had written to Art Fulford. The caller told me that I was talking with "your brother Rick." He explained that dad suspected he had another child, but thought it was a girl. That was why he asked for Donna. He believed that the child has been born on the east coast, so some of the facts were correct! Rick asked if I wanted to speak with my father. My quest had finally ended.

We talked for over an hour the first time, and again several times over the next few weeks. The family was anxious for me to travel to

Ontario so that we could finally meet and be reunited. Although a bit apprehensive—things were happening so fast—I arranged for some vacation time and decided I would go to Ontario. I telephoned dad to tell him of my plans and before I could confirm my air reservations, he had purchased the return ticket and had it delivered to me by courier. There was no turning back. This gesture alone was one of acceptance.

My wife and children were happy for me, but also concerned. They had seen me be hurt and disappointed many times after I had found my mother, and they were afraid that history might repeat itself. I had already decided to go alone. If it turned out to be a disappointment then they would be protected; if it turned out to be what I was hoping for, I was afraid they would feel ignored.

Although I thought I was prepared, when I arrived in Toronto, I almost panicked. What if it didn't work out? My brother Rick, and sister-in-law Fran were waiting for me at Arrivals. Dad had sent me some pictures, so I was able to recognize Rick. Except for his beard, he was almost a mirror reflection of myself. We shared hugs and kisses, and I knew I had made the right decision. The drive home was full of questions and information sharing. It was overwhelming. They had only one person to find out about—I had eight brothers and sisters and a father to get to know! To think that I grew up an only child, and now, between both families, I had thirteen brothers and sisters, plus one brother who had died several years previous.

When I embraced my dad, I felt such a feeling of completeness and peace that I can't describe it. I had not only found my father, I had found myself. I stayed in Ontario for a week and met all of my brothers and sisters and their families. I genuinely felt that I was one of them. I met them on a one-to-one basis, which was much easier than all at once. There were a couple of very special occasions. For those who grow up with brothers and sisters, some of the little things that happen are taken for granted. While I was in Ontario, there was a homebuilding show in one of the neighbouring communities. Two of my brothers, Rick and Ken, decided that it would be fun to go, so the three of us got in the car and away we went. No one will ever know how much fun that was for me, to be doing something like this with "my brothers." For them, this was a normal thing to do; for me, it was like a secret wish had come true. Another time, while

Bob and
birth father,
Arthur Fulford
—reunited
April 9, 1990.

Bob reunited with maternal birth
sisters, Debbie, Fran, Pat and Vicki—
April 1990.

Bob and brother, Rick (Fulford),
at monument dedication—
August 31, 1997.

visiting the campsite where the family used to spend their vacations, my brother Ken and I went for a walk around the campground. We talked about what it was like when they were growing up here. I could almost imagine myself being there with them. It was also sad, as I became aware of things that I had missed out on. On Sunday, a few days before I returned home, all my brothers and sisters and their children came to my father's to officially welcome me into the family. It was an exciting day, and although I was the reason for the family gathering, I enjoyed just sitting back and watching their interaction as a family.

While in Ontario, I met my sisters on my birth mother's side of the family (at this point, I had only met Penny). One of my sisters, Pat, had arranged a gathering to finally meet me. I wasn't sure that I was up to this, as I still had a sense of rejection from my mother's family. My sister Sharon (on dad's side of the family) knew Pat, and she offered to come with me. We were all a bit nervous, but Pat had prepared enough food to feed the neighbourhood, and did everything possible to make sure that everything was just perfect. All my sisters were there, except for Penny, who was living out west, but she sent a special video to be played while I was there. It was difficult to read everyone's reactions to me. I know it was difficult for my younger sister, Vicki. She found it hard to believe that our mother could have had another child and given him up. I have had no contact with either Debbie and Vicki since that meeting. I regret it, but it is nothing that I can change. I will always be here should they decide that I have a place in their lives. I also met Fran's son Ken (my nephew), while at the gathering. We bonded instantly and have become the best of friends, visiting back and forth many times. He is a very special part of my family. It was through Kenny and my dad that I really learned more about my mother, and I found some of the peace that was missing when I thought of her. I wish I had met them when I first found her. I believe that we would have developed a much stronger relationship.

The week in Ontario was an emotional roller coaster for me. I had always been able to keep my emotions under control, but was now dealing with many different and new ones. I was anxious to be back home with my wife and children, but I didn't feel ready to leave my new family behind. I was afraid if I left this dream it would end, and I would never see any of them again. I couldn't control the tears as I watched Rick and Fran walk away from the departure area at the airport. As I waited to board the plane, I had such an empty feeling, the likes of which I have never experienced before. I was anxious to get home to share everything with Donna and the kids, but I wanted my new family too.

When I got home, I had to decide how to tell mom about finding dad and about my trip to Ontario. I wasn't anticipating the same reaction as when I had found Violet, but was still apprehensive. It was easier than expected. She was genuinely excited and wanted to know all of the details and to see my pictures. She was amazed at the similarity between dad and me. There was no denying that he was my father. Mom asked for his address. This really surprised me, but I gave it to her, without knowing if she would ever make contact with him.

In fact, mom and dad corresponded regularly through mail and by telephone. They got along quite well, and mom actually planned to see dad while she was visiting a friend in Ontario!

Needless to say, I was really pleased. I had never dreamed that they would ever have contact, let alone become friends. Unfortunately, my mom suffered a coronary and died less than two months before the planned visit. Her death was sudden and devastating. It was another hard and tragic time in my life, but being a survivor, I got through it with the love and support of my family. It was strange, but natural, that after calling my wife to tell her my mom had died, I called my dad. I really needed to know that he was there for me—and he was. When I was going through some of mom's things I came across some letters she and my dad had exchanged. One in particular referred to me as "their son" and both of them mentioned being pleased at how I turned out. What a beautiful thing to find; the pleasure that I got from reading those words was immeasurable.

That was seven years ago, and, sadly, my dad is now gone. I miss him dearly, but thank God that we had five years to get to know each other. He once said to me, "You know, we are lucky, we have had the best of both worlds. You have had your family, and I have had my family, and now we have found each other."

Rick and Fran, as well as Ken and Judi, first came to Nova Scotia to attend my daughter's wedding. That made a very special day even more special. Rick and Fran were also here for the Survivors' reunion and monument dedication in August 1997. Rick said that when he found out that there would be families coming together, some for the first time, he thought it only right that he be there with me. I was so pleased and proud to have him here and to introduce him to my new and old friends.

Over the past seven years, I have met many aunts, uncles, cousins, nieces, and nephews. My nephew Ken comes to Nova Scotia several times a year, and I still write and telephone some of my other brothers and sisters.

I feel blessed that I have found my biological family, but although important, they could never replace my adoptive family, particularly my mother. She was a caring and loving person who gave of herself every day of her life to me and my family. We will always miss her. And my adoptive dad left me with wonderful memories of my early childhood. It is ironic that my adoptive mom and my birth dad became such special people in my life and also become friends with each other.

I only got to know one small side of my birth mother while she was alive. There were times that I felt angry and frustrated with our relationship, but I also felt love. Sometimes I regret not meeting her, but I think it was the right decision. I never intended to disrupt her life or anyone else's in searching for them. I regret that when I did come back into her life, I opened old wounds. I do believe that when my birth mother died, it was with a clearer conscience, and satisfaction in the knowledge that she was forgiven for the decision made so many years ago, and loved by the son she was forced to give up at birth. Even though I wasn't with her in the end, a symbol of my love—a single rose—was placed beside her on her final journey. I owe her the gift of life.

Today, I have a wonderful and supportive wife, Donna, a daughter, Dawn, her husband, Jamie, and a beautiful granddaughter, Meghan. I also have a son, Robert, his wife, Tracy, and another beautiful granddaughter, Samantha. Although I have lost all four of my parents, Donna's mother, Evelyn, is like a mother to me.

It was with the love and support of my family that I was able to make and fulfill a commitment to re-establish the Survivors group started by Michael Reider, to continue to find more Survivors and to hopefully facilitate their reunion with their biological families—and each other.

Truth in My Roots

JOE BELLEFONTAINE

On a cloudy August 11, 1942, at 3:28 P.M., I was born at the Grace Maternity Hospital in Halifax, Nova Scotia. Within days of my birth, my mother placed me in the care of the Ideal Maternity Home in East Chester, Nova Scotia.

Sixteen and a half months later, I was adopted by Julia and Joseph Bellefontaine from West Chezzetcook, Nova Scotia. My adopted mother had two miscarriages, and because of the danger to her own health, was advised to adopt a child, rather than risk childbirth again. They were the greatest parents one could have. An older couple in their mid forties, they ran a well-known general store in West Chezzetcook. Although the business kept them busy, they always found time for me. Being an only child, I received all the attention and, of course, was somewhat spoiled.

When I was about seven years old, my mother told me that I had been adopted. She told me that my birth mother was a thirty-nine-year-old school teacher from West L'Ardoise, Cape Breton, Nova Scotia, named May Mombourquette. May was unable to look after me, so she placed me for adoption at the Ideal Maternity Home, requesting that I be placed in a good Catholic home. I am grateful that my mother was so honest with me; it proved to me how much she loved me. That day, the seed for knowing my roots was planted. Even though I loved my adopted mother and dad very much, I longed to know my birth mom and dad.

I carried that feeling through all my teenage years. The yearning to know who you are can only be fully understood by someone who has walked that path. As hard as I tried to keep this desire to myself, my adopted parents were aware of my internal turmoil, but they never regretted telling me about my birth mother. I prepared myself for the day I would meet my birth mom, which finally arrived in 1969, twenty years after I had been told of my adoption.

From the mid to the late 60s, I did my own detective work—it took me three years to finally locate my birth mother. I knew that my birth mother was born on March 14, 1903, in the community of West L'Ardoise, Cape Breton. She never married, and taught school in her home community for about six years, leaving before I was born and returning in the mid 1980s. In 1995, she moved to Richmond Villa in St. Peter's, Cape Breton.

First, I contacted every person named Mombourquette in Halifax and Dartmouth, and talked to people in West L'Ardoise. I knew that bringing up the past can be upsetting, especially for older people, but I had to know about my mother. The people in that community did not realize that I understand Acadian French and could understand their conversations. For instance, in the little grocery store I visited to ask about my mother, the locals cautioned each other in French to say nothing. This confirmed that I was on the right track. I visited a lady with the same name as my mother, who was also a school teacher. She assured me that she was not my mother. I went to the graveyard to check for names and then visited the local priest. Back home in West Chezzetcook, with my new information, I re-contacted a woman who I believed knew about my mother. As soon as she saw me, she said in French, "It's him, it's just like she spit him out of her mouth." That's an old French expression. She told me that she had last seen my mother in 1942, on a city tram car in Halifax, when she was pregnant. She said, "People in those days kept it quiet because of the shame that was brought to the family, the community, and the church."

Now that I knew for certain who she was, the time had come to meet her. Later that week, I went to her workplace in Halifax, looked her in the eyes and said, "I am looking for May Mombourquette." She replied, "I am her, what can I do for you?" "My name is Joe Mombourquette," I replied, "and I'm looking for my mother." She turned white, and as we continued to stare at each other, she said that it would be better to meet her after work.

Joe at 18 months old (1944).

Joe

May Mombourquette—Joe's birth mother.

I wanted to visit her at her home, but she was not comfortable with that, so we met at a restaurant and had supper together. I was candid with her, and showed her pictures of my wife and two boys. I explained to her that I just wanted to meet my mother and to let her know that I was all right. I also told her that I wasn't there to pass judgement. Despite being completely honest and open with her, she only said, "I'll see what I can do for you. I'll speak to a friend who may know something." I didn't respond.

I wanted to tell her that I knew unequivocally that she was my mother. I suspected that if she admitted to being my mother, she feared my next question would be even harder: "Who is my father?" It was clear that my mother did not want to face the painful memories that acknowledging me would bring. She had one brother who was very protective, so I could not appeal to him. I did contact the priest and archbishop in Halifax, but they were not willing to get involved. I had run out of options.

Twenty-five years later, on June 11, 1994, I arrived in my mother's hometown at about 2:30 P.M. I went straight to the rectory to talk with Father MacDonald about how to bring about a reunion. After I had finally connected with Parent Finders and got the help I needed to renew my efforts to reunite with my birth mother, I had prepared a letter for my mother, and Father MacDonald asked me if he could see it. Actually, I had prepared three sealed letters, and one unsealed, which I gave him, along with one of the sealed ones. The extra copy was my insurance, in case I was unsuccessful in delivering it to my mother. The other letters were to be mailed and one sent by courier to her home if all else failed.

After Father MacDonald read the letter, he said, "Joe, take this letter to your mother. Leave it with her, and ask her to read it. Let her know that she can contact you back here at the rectory." We prayed together before I walked across the street, feeling hope for my long-awaited reunion with my birth mother.

My uncle answered my knock. I told him that I wanted to see his sister May. He said she was resting, and asked: "Who are you, and what can I do?" I told him my name, and said that I had a letter for May and that I had instructions to deliver it to her in person. "I'm leaving for Halifax within the hour. I'm sure that your sister will be very disappointed if she doesn't have the opportunity to read this important letter," I said. He left the room and within a few minutes a fragile little woman with a warm smile appeared. She did not recognize me from our meeting long ago and asked, "Who are you?"

As soon as I told her my name, she knew. "I am not here to bother or upset you, but I have a very important letter that I would like to leave with you to read. I will be at the rectory until 4 P.M. If you wish to discuss or ask me any questions about this letter, please contact me there." She agreed, and I returned to the rectory to wait. Father MacDonald kept looking at his watch and saying, "I hope she's going to call." The longest forty minutes I have ever endured went by.

Then the phone rang. "It's your mother, she wants you to go over," Father MacDonald exclaimed. I couldn't hold back any longer; the tears flowed. I didn't want my mother to see me like that but he urged me to go. "Let her see you like that, go now," he said.

Both my mother and my uncle greeted me at the door. Mother told me about my birth. She said at the time there was no way she could look after me. The Catholic Home of the Guardian Angel would only look after her if she quit her job and stayed home with me, but she had to earn a living. She had no choice but to place me in the Ideal Maternity Home. She paid for my board for sixteen and a half months, not knowing that the abnormal confinement and lack of socialization would affect my ability to walk and my mental well-being. She told me that she had wanted to find me, but Lila Young swore her to secrecy and made her promise never to look for me. Her lips were sealed until this day.

Father MacDonald stopped by to chat with us for a while. My mother was pleased to hear that I had been married in the church. She asked about my sons and I showed her their pictures. When I gave her my business card, she said, "Bellefontaine Photography. Didn't you tell me twenty-five years ago that you fixed TVs, when you gave me your business card?" She did remember. Mother asked me if I wanted the letter back, but I told her that it was for her to keep. She said, "Yes, yes," when I asked if I could come again. This was the reply I was waiting to hear. I told her that I was now the happiest person on earth. Before I left, I hugged and kissed my birth mother for the first time. She thanked me for coming. Words can never express the wonderful feeling I experienced on being acknowledged by her.

Later that evening, I met with Father MacDonald, who was delighted that our reunion had gone so well. I was "floating on a cloud." I found out that Father MacDonald was leaving the parish at the end of June, and was grateful that I got there before he left. Without his help, the chances of reuniting with my mother would have been lessened. I am also grateful to Mike Slayter of Parent Finders, Nova Scotia, for his helpful suggestion during my first meeting at the organization in May 1994.

My birth mother passed away on March 11, 1998—three days before her ninety-fifth birthday, and only a few short hours before I arrived to be at her side. I volunteered to be a pallbearer at her funeral, feeling that this was the least I could do to show my gratitude for the life she had given me. We had come full circle and I could now lay my mom to rest. (My adoptive dad had died on July 13, 1960, and I lost my adoptive mom on November 30, 1976.)

Being one of the Butterbox Baby Survivors, I continue to carry the vivid conscious and unconscious memories of physical and mental abuse that occurred at the Ideal Maternity Home. These memories will stay with some of us for the rest of our lives.

I am thankful for the wonderful home and love my adopted parents gave me. I only wish that the hundreds of babies who became known as the Butterbox Babies had been given the same chance to live. My heart breaks for my mother, who carried needless guilt and shame for fifty-six years.

The Circle of Love

RON MURDOCK

$\mathcal{J}$ was born Ronald Anthony Arab at the Ideal Maternity Home on February 9, 1941. I lived there for the first seven months of my life until I was rescued by my adoptive mother, Kaye Murdock. She came to the Home with a group of ladies from Merigomish, including her best friend, who was intending to adopt a baby. Mum had not discussed adoption with her husband, Russell—my new father to be—although he did say as she left for the day, "Don't do anything foolish."

While she was waiting for her friend to complete the formalities of adopting her chosen baby, Mum wandered around the place looking at all the babies in their cots. When she came to mine I reached out to her and she picked me up. She fell in love with me on the spot and took me home that same day. For the past fifty-seven years her love for me has always been there.

On the drive back home she began to panic, worried if she had done the right thing. The other women, who knew my dad, assured her he would accept me just as she had. When she walked in the house, dad asked, "What have you got here?" "It's a little boy," she said. "What a little darling," he replied as he opened his arms and wrapped me in them. I was home.

Mum and dad followed through with adoption proceedings and I grew up as part of the Murdock family. There was my sister, Bonnie (their own child by birth), and all the close-knit Murdock clan, made up of my father's brothers, sisters, and their many children. I never once felt that I didn't belong. I owe whatever I am today to their love. It was my mother who encouraged me to follow my love of music. It was she who sang to me and who, while she was singing to me, made me feel so special.

There are two churches in the village of Merigomish, where I grew up. My mother attended the Presbyterian Church. It was here that I had my first public singing experience, at the age of four. The hymn was "Jesus Bids Us Shine," which I sang while holding a lighted candle—my hand trembling so much that the candle blew out. As a teenager, I joined the choir, which sang every Sunday. In 1989, I gave two recitals to mark the 200th anniversary of the founding of the church.

My high school music teacher, Eleanor Sutherland, introduced me to the symphony music of Mozart, Beethoven, Schumann, and Schubert, as well as to the songs of Schubert. She let me borrow the records so I could listen to them at home. I will never forget the thrill of hearing those works for the first time. I spent hours listening to Saturday afternoon performances from the Metropolitan Opera in New York. One evening I heard Handel's *Messiah*. The music thrilled and excited me so much that I didn't sleep for nights afterward.

At the beginning of grade ten, my best friend Marion Mason began having singing lessons with Vivian Brand in New Glasgow. This seemed like a good idea so I asked Mrs. Sutherland if she would approach Vivian for me. It was love at first sight, not only of singing, but of Vivian herself. She coached and taught me basic principles of singing and brought out my natural musicianship. Marion and I sang together in almost every church in Pictou County, at numerous weddings, and whenever the two of us were together.

After three years of study with Vivian, I won every voice class in the New Glasgow Music Festival. The adjudicator that year was Dr. Leslie Bell, the famous conductor of the Leslie Bell Singers in Toronto. He offered to take me under his wing in Toronto and make me a folk singing star on TV, but I wanted to pursue a classical music career and get a university education, so I declined his kind offer. I graduated from Mount Allison University in Sackville, New Brunswick, in 1962, with a Bachelor of Arts degree and Associateship in Music Diploma.

After graduating, I earned the first of many scholarships from the Nova Scotia Talent Trust, which helped me to study privately in Montreal with Bernard Diemant, the leading voice teacher in Canada. I subsidized my private study in Montreal by teaching school music. While there I became reacquainted with Diana, a young woman I had dated at university. We were married in 1965 in Montreal.

In 1964, the Nova Scotia Talent Trust invited me to give a series of summer concerts with a young soprano, Annon Lee Silver from Glace Bay (also a graduate of Mount Allison University). She was studying in Switzerland with Professor Frederick Husler and Yvonne Rodd Marling. When I heard Annon Lee sing, I knew instantly that I had to go to Switzerland and study with her teachers. On August 24, 1966, Diana and I set out by ship from Montreal, bound for Switzerland by way of Amsterdam. Again, a scholarship from the Nova Scotia Talent Trust (my fifth in a row) paid for the lessons, while we used savings and financial gifts from family and friends to pay travel and living expenses for one year.

I worked well with Husler and Rodd Marling; after three months I had a job with the chorus of Radio Lugano (which paid very well indeed), and as luck would have it, both Diana and I found work at the American School in the next village. I conducted their school choir and taught music history; Diana became secretary to the Dean of the school.

At the beginning of my third year in Switzerland, an audition for the Arts Council of Great Britain landed me a healthy scholarship. I won a music competition organized by the Royal Over-Seas League in London, who sponsored me in several concerts. Because of their interest and encouragement, I went to live in London in 1969. Through them, I was presented to the Queen, and sang for Princess Alexandra at St. James's Palace.

After three wonderful years of marriage, Diana and I lost a baby in the seventh month of pregnancy in November 1968. Diana was shopping in Lugano with a friend when she tripped and fell. She was rushed to hospital, where she was told the baby had died. We had to wait four agonizing days before the baby was stillborn, and in the process, Diana also nearly died. As a couple we never really recovered from that tragedy.

In January 1969, Husler, my teacher and mentor, died. I felt utterly devastated. Still feeling bereft after the loss of the baby and the strain in our marriage, the loss of my Professor before I had completed my studies was almost more than I could bear. But I kept on singing.

In November, we received word that my father had suffered a

massive heart attack. I rushed home not knowing if, when I got there, he would still be alive. Fortunately, he did survive, and I stayed with him and mum for three weeks. Once he got out of intensive care, I was with him every day in hospital. I would quietly sit with him, making sure he was comfortable, shaving him, putting cream on his face to keep it from drying out, and generally just helping him heal. The bond between us, which had always been there, really strengthened. It was a very special time—a time I shall always treasure.

When I returned to London, a series of solo recitals at the Wigmore Hall and the Purcell Room in London brought me to the attention of the London critical press and to a wider audience over the next two years. Agents became interested in my work, began to get jobs for me, and my career took off. I began to record recitals for BBC Radio 3, and returned to Canada to give concerts and recitals in Halifax, Montreal, and Toronto. Radio Zurich and Radio Lugano offered several engagements. There were also engagements in Tel Aviv, Jerusalem, Warsaw, Hong Kong, and throughout the UK.

As our financial situation improved, Diana and I began to think about starting a family again. Our marriage was stronger, and seven years had passed since we lost our first baby; it was time to start again. Our family doctor referred Diana to an excellent gynecologist, Dr. George Pinker, who shepherded us through the pregnancy with great care. He was aware of the trauma we had experienced, and he resolved that this time all would go well.

Our son, Andrew, was born February 19, 1976, at 5 P.M. The following morning, the pediatrician asked Diana what she knew about Downs Syndrome. When I heard the news, I raced to the hospital. We held each other and wept. Andrew lay in his little cot, looking up at me as if to say, "Well, how are you going to deal with this?" He had the brightest pair of eyes I have ever seen in a newborn, and that gave me some hope. Dr. Pinker came in and wept with us. He felt that he had completely failed us. He could have ordered a test for Downs Syndrome during the third month of pregnancy. Diana was only thirty-five at the time and he didn't consider her to be a risk. I am so glad he didn't order that test.

At one of the early meetings with the pediatrician, we were asked if there was any history of Downs Syndrome in our families. I could not answer the question. I explained that I was adopted and had no idea what my family history was because of the Nova Scotia Government's law on nondisclosure of information.

It was hard enough having to deal with the fact that our child was handicapped without having the added embarrassment and frustration of not knowing this vital information. It was at that precise moment that I began to question who I was. Until then, I had not really needed to know. Now I did. I applied for my "non-identifying" identification, and asked to be placed on the Register requesting contact with my parents in case they might be looking for me. The information I received told me nothing I did not already know.

At six months of age, Andrew weighed only ten pounds; it was not clear whether he would survive or not. He was "skin and bones," but had a huge spirit that shone out of his beautiful eyes. I often said he had just enough physical attributes to hold his soul together.

Considering his physical condition, we decided to take him home to Nova Scotia to see his grandparents. When my father saw Andrew for the first time, he said, "Well, there's not much to him is there?" He picked him up, held him close, and Andrew was also "home." For the three weeks we were in Nova Scotia, Andrew spent most of his waking hours lying on my father's chest, held there securely by his strong hands. He sang to him, talked to him, played with him, and when we returned to London, Andrew began to gain weight. Within two months after our return, he weighed twenty pounds. It was now clear that Andrew had decided to stay with us, and today he is a healthy, strong, loving man of twenty-two years, of whom I am justifiably proud.

What was obvious to me during that visit to Nova Scotia was that Andrew had received the same acceptance that I had received from my mother and father and the whole Murdock family. It was wonderful to witness it, experience it all again, and to realize how very lucky he and I had been.

In the fall of 1983, Diana told me she wanted a divorce. In many ways she was the one with her finger on reality. I somehow thought we might still make it, even though it was clear we couldn't. My singing career had nose-dived during the five-year period after Andrew was born. I couldn't face standing in front of an audience, and cancelled one engagement after another, which doesn't do one's reputation any good. Gradually, agents got fed up with me and didn't offer me any work.

I began training to be a teacher of the Alexander Technique in January 1976. By 1979, I had qualified and had a large practice of young professional singers who wanted to study singing and the Alexander Technique with me. In 1981, I was invited to Amsterdam to work with singers there. By 1983, I was teaching full time and enjoying it.

Still, I really needed help, and began sessions with a therapist. Prompted by my therapist, I made contact with the woman whose name is on my adoption papers as being my mother. She was the right age, had the right name, and the right ethnic background, but still denied being my mother. I could go no further without concrete proof from the Nova Scotia Adoption Disclosure Services, which was not forthcoming. The rejection by her set me back years. I was completely devastated. I became depressed and lonely, and felt I would never be able to get out from under the weight of feeling so utterly wretched. Before long, I had a total nervous breakdown, again sought help (where clearly none was available), and suffered another breakdown. Although I didn't know it then, these attempts to find help were desperate attempts to find myself.

In the autumn of 1988, an American horn player in the Concertgebouw orchestra came to me for Alexander lessons following the birth of her daughter. I was attracted to this exceptional woman, but kept my feelings to myself.

Five years later, while having dinner with a mutual friend in Amsterdam, he asked me if I knew that Sharon and her husband were divorced. I called her before he finished speaking.

The following month I was in Amsterdam again and took her out to dinner. When I told her how I felt, she was blown over by the intensity of feeling. "I'm not ready for this," she said. "Take all the time you want; I'm not going anywhere," I replied.

My second breakdown happened just after Sharon and I began our relationship. I had lost confidence in my therapist, and friends in London recommended a Canadian therapist, who helped me heal myself, and discover the answers to some of the questions and self-doubt that raged inside me. It was a case of starting at the beginning and rebuilding my life.

Over a two-year period, I began to deal with my feelings and be more accepting of myself. Sharon helped immeasurably by constantly affirming her love for me and faith in me. The more I was able to be there for myself, the more I wanted to sing. Eventually, my confidence returned, and I resumed teaching. We settled in Amsterdam, and I went to London a week each month to teach, and to see my therapist.

In the summer of 1995, Sharon and I were married in the Merigomish Presbyterian Church, which held so many special memories for me. It was a wonderful and special day with just our family and a few close friends. My old friend Marion, with whom I had sung so many times, sang for us. It was very special to have my son, Andrew, and Sharon's daughter, Nicole—our children—in attendance.

On June 3, 1996, at about one in the morning, our daughter Esther was born at home. She was a beautiful baby, with a full head of very dark hair. It was an unbelievable experience to wake up the next morning with her between us. She slept in our bed for three months before we put her in her own crib. She is now a two-year-old chatterbox, whose first English words (Dutch is her first language) were "I like this song."

In January 1998, I contacted Bob Hartlen after receiving a newsletter from my friend Marion about the Survivors of the Ideal Maternity Home. I had already read *Butterbox Babies* and seen the film. To raise money for the organization, we decided to do a benefit concert to celebrate our adoptive families. It included the collaboration of thirteen actors from Downstage Productions, under the direction of John Frederick Brown, a playwright from Dartmouth. The actors read

Ronald Murdock

the stories of thirteen Survivors from the Home, mine included. I chose songs that reflected the mood and spirit of the texts. It wasn't an easy job singing after some of the stories, and I had to fight back tears; it was a very special event and one I was very proud to take part in.

I am still searching in the hope that one day I may find my birth parents, but it is a different sort of searching than I did before. I no longer need the information to establish who I am. I just want to know for the sake of knowing.

It has been quite a journey, from the Ideal Maternity Home in East Chester, to Merigomish, then Europe, and back again. None of it would have been possible without the tremendous love and acceptance I received from my adopted parents, my sister, and the whole Murdock clan, and now from my wife and children.

It is true what they say about the Circle of Love. It does go around. It does make miracles happen. With love, a bad beginning can lead to human triumph.

Contact!

JERRY RANDALL

During World War II, life was difficult for most people in Nova Scotia, as elsewhere, and rumours about babies being sold on the black market in the U.S.A. from a remote rural orphanage were of little interest to anyone. Everyone was preoccupied with "the boys overseas," and the effort to "keep the home fires burning," for their return.

But the rumours persisted, and the provincial government of the day finally launched an investigation into the practices of the Ideal Maternity Home in East Chester, Lunenburg County. Investigators were assigned to look at the possible criminal implications of adoptions, and one man, Sinclair Randall, was assigned to uncover proof of baby sales. During his investigation, he met me, and eventually became my father.

Sinclair Albert was one of two sons of Captain Morris and Mary Randall of Upper LaHave, Lunenburg County. He married Alice Hilda (nee Armstrong), one of twelve children of Morris and Mamie Armstrong of Mariott's Cove, Lunenburg County. Alice could not have children, so they decided to adopt.

When Sinclair visited the Ideal Maternity Home in 1943, he found a room filled with rows of cribs, each containing a child that was to be placed for adoption. He walked up and down the rows, looking at each child, until he reached my crib. I was standing at the foot of my crib, arms outstretched. I had shoulder-length ringlets, and a cherubic face; he said I was the most beautiful baby in the room. When he returned home to MacDonald Street in Halifax's south end, he told my mother about me. Later, he borrowed a car from a Mr. Kaulback, principal of the Maritime Business College, where my father also worked as a teacher, to take my mother to East Chester to meet me. But before that, while he

was still involved in the investigation at the Home, he had come across my file. He was not supposed to have access to personal information about the children, but he naturally couldn't resist reading it. If it hadn't been for bad luck, he wouldn't have had any luck at all—he got caught by an official from the Home, and the file was taken from him, never to be seen again. During his brief glance, he had learned the name of my birth mother, and her father's name and address—information that would later prove to be very valuable.

Jerry Randall as a child.

After meeting me, mother agreed with father, and they decided to adopt me, so one night, when father was returning to Halifax from the South Shore in Mr. Kaulback's car, he stopped at the Home to pick me up. I was eleven months old, and wearing only diapers and an undershirt. Father stopped at a store in East Chester to buy me some clothes to wear on the journey to Halifax, some three hours away. He also picked up a sailor hitch-hiking back to his ship, who held me for the whole journey.

Mother was out visiting a neighbour, but came as soon as she heard we had arrived. I was lucky! I had been adopted, I had a family, and I was home! Only years later was it learned that many babies from the Home never had that privilege—they became known as "Butterbox Babies," after the boxes used for their coffins. Father told me that the province of Nova Scotia paid a support subsidy to orphanages for babies under a year old. After that subsidy was dropped, the baby often "disappeared." This was apparently the source of the rumours that had created the investigation at the Home in the first place. Since I was eleven months old at the time of my adoption, I was perhaps lucky indeed.

My birth mother's name was Hilda MacEachern. She was from Charlottetown, where her father, a retired policeman, worked at a funeral home. There was no mention of my birth father on the papers my father saw, and I suspect I'll never know who he was. I always thought of myself as "chosen," rather than my parents having to "take what they got."

When I was four or five years old, our family went to PEI on vacation, and father went to the funeral home and made contact with my birth grandfather. I remember sitting on this big man's knee, on the verandah of a building with big white columns. Father didn't tell him I was his grandson, and now mother wonders if they should have. It's too late now!

I grew up in a loving, nurturing environment. When I was little, we moved to Lunenburg, where my father had taken the job of Municipal Clerk-Treasurer for Lunenburg County. I was given every privilege and opportunity to reach my potential, and although I didn't always take advantage of them, I couldn't imagine having a better home with better parents. Everyone treated me as a full family member, and my adoption was never an issue. But I always felt I was different from my cousins. My father's brother married my mother's sister, and when I was with my cousins, I didn't feel a genetic connection—I had different talents and interests. Still, I had little interest in my past, and it has only been in the last few years that I've become interested in genealogy. Much of my interest was sparked by my daughter, who has a unique medical condition, which made her wonder if it was genetically triggered. She thought if I could find my family, it might shed some light on her health.

In November 1996, I contacted Prince Edward Island's Department of Vital Statistics, requesting information on Hilda MacEachern. I received a phone call from a Ritchie Mayne of PEI Post-Adoption Services, who told me that if I could prove that the Hilda MacEachern I knew was my mother was the same Hilda MacEachern they had on file, she had information she could share with me. She also said that Hilda MacEachern had at least two other children, both female, and that one was trying to make contact with any known siblings.

I contacted Nova Scotia's Department of Vital Statistics for information on my birth name, Sydney Benjamin MacEachern, which I thought would include information about my birth mother. There was no birth record under that name.

In November 1997, I wrote again to PEI, requesting information about birth dates, and was told that I should contact Ritchie Mayne, after she returned from an extended vacation on January 14. I called on that date, and received a flood of information that left me sitting with my mouth open.

Ritchie already had the proof she needed to confirm that my mother was one of five daughters of Susan and Benjamin (after whom I was obviously named) MacEachern of Charlottetown. Hilda was born in 1920. She had given birth to a total of six children, and I was the oldest, being born February 24, 1943. Richard, born next in 1946, was adopted by his grandparents. He grew up in the MacEachern family, and until age fourteen, thought of his grandparents as his parents. He met Hilda on two occasions, the first as his sister, and the second, at age fourteen, as his mother. When Richard's grandfather died, he moved with his grandmother to Ontario. He is now living in Pickering, where he works at Ontario Hydro's nuclear plant.

Hilda had a daughter, Sandra, in 1948, who was put up for adoption and went to live in O'Leary, PEI, with the late Dorothy and Herbert Dennis, who changed her name to Phyllis. She had made the inquiry I had been told about in 1996. She has lived in Ontario—also currently in Pickering—since she was twenty. Richard discovered her existence when he visited PEI Post-Adoption Services in the summer of 1997, seeking information on his birth father, whose name he knew. Coincidentally, his visit occurred on the same day that Ritchie was trying to contact him in Ontario. When he discovered that he had a sister living in his home town, he cut his vacation short, and went straight to Phyllis. They've been in close touch ever since.

Hilda had another daughter, named Susan at birth, born in August 1951, in PEI. There were also two sons, born in Nova Scotia in 1955 and 1956. The good news was that Phyllis and Richard were anxious to contact me.

Although I had no interest in meeting Hilda, I was somewhat intrigued by the possibility of meeting blood relatives. By January 1998, the idea of making contact with a half-sister and half-brother had become decidedly exciting, so I told Ritchie to let Phyllis and Richard know they could contact me.

A phone call at about 8:77 P.M., and the words, "Hi! Jerry? Phyllis here," brought my sporadic search to a close. Richard was with her, and we talked for an hour or so. He is a great source of information, since he grew up in the MacEachern family.

Richard has photos of my birth mother and grandparents. He confirmed my memory of the columns in front of the Cutcliffe Funeral Home, where he often played in the coffin loft as a child. Now I have an emotional tie to the MacEachern side of my heritage.

Jerry Randall,
Town-crier for Amherst, NS.

Phyllis called me again on February 6, 1998, to say she had made contact with Susan, our other sibling in PEI. I contacted here at once. She lives in Charlottetown, and is named Inez Waddell. She grew up with an alcoholic mother and a father who was some thirty years older than her mother. When her father died, her mother was too drunk to take care of funeral arrangements, leaving Inez, at the age of twelve, responsible. Inez only discovered that she was adopted when her aunt told her it was her mother's dying wish that she know. Inez was nineteen at the time. She has married twice, and divorced twice, and has two sons, one from each husband. One son lives in PEI, and the other in British Columbia. Inez operates a boarding home in Charlottetown, where my wife, daughter, and I visited her in February 1998. We discovered that we are both reserved about our family relationships, and want to take things slowly. I do find her sense of humour delightful. She said she had decided that if she didn't like us she would simply ask us for a loan. She figured that would get rid of us pretty quickly. Fortunately, that hasn't happened, and we have spoken on several occasions since our meeting.

Richard and Phyllis are planning a trip to Charlottetown, when we will all meet at the same time. It will be an interesting meeting, and one I'm sure will strengthen our friendship, if not the brother/sister relationships, with which I am still uncomfortable. Either way, the contact has been rewarding, and I'm pleased it happened.

My two half-brothers are most likely living somewhere in Nova Scotia. I have begun a search for them through the Nova Scotia Adoption Services Disclosures Program in Halifax. It would be nice if all six of us could be together when Phyllis and Richard arrive.

Hilda MacEachern died on November 28, 1980, in a nursing home near Toronto, and two of her sisters have also died. Two are still living, one suffering from Alzheimer's disease in a nursing home in Ontario, and the other, Lois, also living in Ontario. She has had a lifetime of contact with Richard, has now met Phyllis, and may someday meet me and maybe even the others. She too is a source of family information that may help to fill in some gray areas.

It is quite obvious that Hilda lived a less than stellar life, and the tendency to judge her harshly could be easy. As a severe alcoholic, her life was probably difficult, more so since the disease was much less tolerated or treatable in her time. Alcoholism leaves little by way of personal choice, and without a strong network of support and help, getting out of it is nearly impossible. I think that must have been the case with her, and I feel very sorry for her. In a way, I have to thank her, for had she not given me up, I would not have enjoyed the life I had with my wonderful parents. Lord only knows where I might have ended up.

My wife and I will celebrate out thirty-first anniversary on May 27, 1998. We have had a wonderful life together, with our two children, Michael and Kristina.

I'll retire from twenty-five years with Corrections Canada in May 1999, and Vicki will retire in January 2001. We plan to follow the sun in winter, and I will fill my days as a freelance journalist, returning to my enduring interest—writing. In 1992, my book, *Handcuffs and Ploughshares, A History of Westmorland Institution and Farming on the Dorchester Penitentiary Property Since 1880*, was published and distributed by Corrections Canada.

My interest in my family history started as a genealogy hobby—a means of adding information to my past. I have a tremendous base of my mother's people (Armstrong) back to the mid 1700s, and of my father's mother's family (Morash/Parks) to the same period. I never dreamed that my hobby would result in finding so many half-brothers and half-sisters. Friends and family are amazed at this development. Frankly, so am I.

Jerry and wife, Vicki.
Jerry is the town crier of
Amherst, NS.

But for the Grace of God...

J O E L

J was born in May 1945, in a hospital in Windsor, Nova Scotia. Following my birth, I was taken to the Ideal Maternity Home in East Chester, where I was left and placed for adoption. I remained there until September 1945, when I was adopted by two loving parents and was taken to their home on the south shore of Nova Scotia, where I was brought up as an only child. My parents told me at an early age that I was adopted, but that I was chosen, and so was special, and that they were very happy to have me. They said I was their child, and should never think of my adoption or my birth parents. Perhaps because of their attitude, I grew to hate the idea of being adopted, and really wanted to be my parents' own flesh and blood. I cringed when my peers in our small community would ask me about adoption. I felt that it made me less of a person, and that thinking about my past was being disloyal to my adopted parents. I hid this secret so well that I even came to believe that I was the natural son of my parents. I didn't discuss my adoption with anyone—not my relatives (one of whom had also been adopted), my children, or even my wife, who, I found out later, had known from the time she met me. Even as a young adult I hated applying for insurance as this brought the doctor's exam, which inevitably included the question, "Have any of these diseases or conditions shown up in your parents?" I did not actively deal with my adoption until I was over fifty years old.

In December 1995, my son, who had been away at university, had to return home due to an illness. My wife and I were very concerned about his health and I began wondering if this illness might have been inherited from my birth mother or father. I gathered up the courage and approached my mother, who is now elderly, for information about my adoption. Reluctantly, she told me that she adopted me from the Ideal Maternity Home. She had no medical history, but gave me two possible given names and the surname of my birth mother, but no name for my birth father; she said she had burned all of my adoption papers. I was shocked, but at the same time I wanted to know even more, and not just for medical purposes but for my own curiosity. I had broken the ice.

In July 1996, I attended a Parent Finders meeting to find out how to search for my birth relatives. I also met a number of people who had experiences that were similar to mine. I learned from these very caring people that I was not being disloyal, was not alone, and had a natural desire that was common to them all. The group suggested that I contact Community Services to make inquiries, which I did. They returned a certificate of adoption to me, confirming that I was adopted from the Home. They said they could not disclose my birth name, birth mother's name, or any identifying information until after January 1, 1997, when new legislation was to be put into place. In the meantime, my wife and I read *Butterbox Babies* repeatedly. We also visited the site of the Home in East Chester, and visited Lila Young's grave and the adjacent baby-burying ground in Fox Point. At this time I talked to a number of Butterbox Survivors, who related many a gruesome tale. There but for the grace of God am I.

One night in late August, I received a call from one of the search leaders, who gave me information regarding my birth mother that really upset me. My birth mother had died and was buried in the Windsor Cemetery. But I did have relatives living in the Valley area. I focused on a nephew and the daughter of the woman who was my possible birth mother. A friend from Parent Finders NS, who lives in the Valley, provided a contact, who gave me a picture of my possible mother and the addresses of the nephew and daughter. In November, I drove to Windsor, visited the family homestead, and talked to a number of people who knew my mother, her brother, and my maternal grandparents. In early December, after much discussion, my wife and I travelled to a Valley town and knocked on the door of a possible cousin. I did not call beforehand, just drove up to the house. When my knock was answered, I introduced my-self, and related my story. My cousin showed me more pictures of the woman I thought might have been my mother and discussed her life, but said he had never heard of his aunt having a child in 1945. She was mar-ried in 1944 but her husband was overseas in the forces until 1946. We spent a lovely afternoon with two very friendly people, but my cousin would not pursue the case with other members of the family until I had proof, which was not available until after January 1997.

In late January 1997, I got a call from a woman who said she was my birth mother's daughter, by her father who had been overseas during the war. She felt that maybe her mother did have a child previously but had no real proof. We arranged a meeting with her and her husband.

Once again we were received as one of the family, but after consider-able discussions there was some doubt whether this woman's mother and mine were the same person. She called Community Services in order to try to help me out. Community Services confirmed that the name I thought was my birth mother's was not the one on my records. A search, more information, or any confirmation, would cost $250.

I went back to my elderly adopted parents and told them my story. My mother then told me that she remembered the correct given names of my birth mother, her approximate age at the time of my adoption, and my two given birth names. I again called Community Services, but they would not confirm the information about my life unless I paid the fee. I became despondent, as I had made so many wild goose chases and, worst of all, had interfered with the families of complete strangers. I wanted off the emotional roller coaster.

In despair, I went back to Parent Finders, and by chance I attended a meeting of the Monument Committee for the Survivors of the Ideal Maternity Home. A woman on the committee (who was also a Survi-vor) became very interested in my story and, from records available to her, confirmed my birth name, and obtained information about a woman who had the same surname and given name as my birth mother. She also provided me with an obituary and family history of my birth mother. I learned that my mother married after I had been born and that she had a son living in a Valley town in Nova Scotia. I sent the $250 fee to Community Services. The search confirmed what I thought was true. My mother's birth names, married names, and my birth name were now fact. Again there was no other medical, historical, or family records recorded. Apparently, Lila Young did not elaborate on anything more than she had to. Ironically, the document held by Social Services was a copy of the original order that my adopted parents had destroyed.

In April 1997, my wife and I journeyed to the Valley, visited my mother's grave, and knocked on the door of my half-brother. I had been warned by a friend of mine from the area that he was a bit of a recluse. The door opened a crack and a man stuck his nose out and asked me what I wanted. I related my story. He was not the least interested and indicated that I should leave. I was dumbfounded; I had been rejected by my blood brother. I felt hurt, angry, and dejected.

After awhile, I looked at the situation more objectively, realizing that this was probably a total shock to my half-brother; he may have not have known about me, and he was known as a recluse. I returned home vowing to write to him, giving him proof of my identity, and leaving my phone number and address if he ever wished to contact me. I still had my mother's nieces and nephews to call. I knew my niece was willing to see me; apparently, she had known that her aunt had a baby that was given up for adoption.

In May, my wife and I ventured to the Valley again to see my cousin. When we arrived, my niece, two nephews, their children, and an older half-niece—who remembered the day that my mother gave birth to me—were waiting for us. They all were aware of my birth but did not know of my birth father or of my placement at the Ideal Maternity Home. Everyone was so friendly; we were treated as family. We spent the entire afternoon viewing pictures, listening to family history, and really getting to know one another. All of the relatives knew my mother and could see how I resembled her. This was quite overwhelming, both for my wife and for me. As we left for home a feeling of nostalgia overcame me—my long search was over. We all made plans to stay in touch and also to visit back and forth as much as possible.

Finding my roots comes at the same time that I am retiring from the teaching profession, having spent thirty-two years as a teacher, school principal, and system supervisor. Even greater than the satisfaction of finding my roots is that I have met so many generous, sincere, and loving human beings. I hope that I have grown as a person and am able to overcome the guilt that I have always felt about adoption. My relationship with my wife has been strengthened by the fact that she was always supportive, if at times bewildered, when encouraging me to press on. I think back to the period before I knew that I had been adopted from the Ideal Maternity Home. Why had I attended a showing of the play *Butterbox Babies*? Why had I rescued a LaHave Creamery butterbox from my wife's home on the death of her mother? Why had I developed a unit on the Home to teach to my class? These were all bizarre events that preceded the search for my adoptive history.

Prior to the 1997 Christmas Season, I decided that our children should meet my new-found family and get to know them. So we took the family for a holiday visit, and all of the cousins and their families gathered at one home. It was a joyous event—one big party and a wonderful welcome for all of us again. We were indeed family. During the party, one of my cousins took me aside and asked, "Would you like a Christmas present? How would you feel knowing that you had a full sister?" I was overwhelmed.

She told me that my mother had another child, a daughter, born two years after me. My mother's pregnancy went undetected, as she was a large woman, and the child was born at home—a secret, right up until the birth. The baby was cared for by an aunt for several months, and was subsequently adopted. My cousin knew my father's name; he was also the father of my sister. Unfortunately he too is deceased, but at least I now know his name, where he lived, and where he was buried.

When I thought my search was completed, I find it is now just beginning again, but this time for my sister—a full blood relative—who is living out there somewhere. As I think about this, I can but wonder where this part of the search will take me.

The Discovery

PETER CHARLES MALONEY

J was born at the Ideal Maternity Home on September 27, 1944, as Samuel Maurice Carr. I had no idea that I was adopted until I was about fifteen years old. I enjoyed a normal childhood, but when I was around seven or eight years old, I started having a recurring dream. It wasn't a scary dream but it was a sad one, which left me with a feeling of loneliness. It happened at least once a month. The dream was so vivid I could draw a picture of it. I was laying on my back and all I could see was the ceiling and part of the walls of a room, and a door frame. There was a long hallway, with round light globes in its white ceiling. The walls were white plaster extending about five feet down from the ceiling, with brown varnished wooden slats from the plaster to the floor. The door frame was made of the same kind of brown varnished wooden slats. I was heading for the door. But the room I was going to was also lonely. That's all I could remember.

One day, when I was about fifteen, coming home from Saint Pat's High School in Halifax, I saw a sign advertising a fudge sale in front of the Home of the Guardian Angels. I loved fudge so I went into the Home to buy some.

It was just like in my dream. There were the same walls, with the same combination of wooden slats and plaster, the same door frames, and the same ceiling, except for long fluorescent lights; the globes had been replaced. I remember feeling terribly confused and I don't know if I bought any fudge or not. After that day, I never had the dream again.

Peter and his sister Mary.

Peter and adoptive family at Christmas.
(L-R) Mother, holding Joseph, Mary,
Peter, and Dad, holding Michael.

Peter at 2 years old (1946).

Peter and Libera on their wedding day
—July 5, 1980.

Peter (1998).

One night shortly after, I needed a pen to do my homework, so I went to my mother's room, and used a key I had made months before, to open her trunk. As I was searching around I noticed an envelope on which the words, "Personal, Do Not Open," were written in large letters. Maybe not all fifteen-year-old kids would have opened it, but I did. What I found changed my life, because in the envelope were my adoption papers.

I read the adoption papers from start to finish about a hundred times before it sunk in that the person whose name had changed from Samuel Maurice Carr to Peter Charles Maloney was *me*! Three other facts stuck in my mind: I needed a dictionary to look up the complex legal terms; I found the "thees" and "thous" reminded me of the King James version of the Bible; and my sister's adoption papers were also in the envelope.

I felt more alone than I had ever felt in my life. It was as though I was back in that lonely room of my dream. I cried but it was a strange kind of crying; I wasn't hurt, I felt no physical pain, no one had hurt my feelings, but I couldn't stop. I had to hide. I didn't know why I was hiding but I felt I had to.

After my discovery, I walked around in a daze for weeks or maybe months. I didn't tell my mom, and there was no dad to tell. He had left when I was seven. He wasn't around much in those early years anyway. He was a sea captain and was at sea all the time. Once in a while this man whom mom called "dad" would show up for a week or so, but I only remember him as a stranger.

Months later, I asked my mom point blank if I was adopted, "Don't be so foolish," she replied, "Where did you hear trash like that?"

When I was about twenty-two and leaving home for my first job, I had to get a copy of my birth certificate. It said I was born in East Chester, Nova Scotia. I asked again if I was adopted and she said "Yes!" I knew by the way she spoke that she wasn't aware that I knew. She wasn't even aware that my adoption papers were in my possession. I still have them today, in a safety deposit box.

She said I was adopted from the Home of the Guardian Angels on Brunswick Street in Halifax, but that I had come from a really bad place— Young's Hotel. Many years later I discovered that Young's Hotel and the Ideal Maternity Home were the same place. She said that my birth mother's brother got me out of there just in time and took me to the

Home of the Guardian Angels when I was two years old. "You never spoke a word," she said, "until you were three years old." They told her at the Home that I was retarded; she told them that they were.

That is the only information I have on my past, but I would like to find out who I am because there is a big empty hole in my heart. It comes to the surface once a year around my birthday. It seems to get worse each year, and sometimes tears run down my face and I feel ashamed without knowing why. Then I push it back for another year. But this year, it won't go away. That's because I have discovered the Canadopt home page on the Internet. Now, of course, I will be accessing the Ideal Maternity Home Page, to see if I can somehow make a contact with my past.

Well, that's my story; another lucky Survivor of the Ideal Maternity Home. I am married to a wonderful wife, and have four boys, two dogs, one cat, and three fish.

Two Names—Half a Story

FRANKLIN THOMAS
RUTHERFORD

J knew nothing of the horror stories associated with the Ideal Maternity Home until I read the book *Butterbox Babies*. I did see the Home though, on a trip with my mother and uncle, while travelling from Bridgewater to Halifax in the mid-50s. I was twelve or thirteen years old at the time, and I can remember the "tower" at the front of the building, and a globe with a baby on the roof.

My mother often told me the story of how they got me, and the trouble they had getting me home over the muddy roads that spring. My dad and mom were just two years into their married life together when they decided to "have a child." I'm not sure how they heard about the Ideal Maternity Home, though I understand that there was a fairly aggressive advertising campaign as late as the mid 1940s. This campaign surfaced as far away as central Canada. The decision being made, they set off to the village of East Chester to find a daughter!

Mom talked very little of the Home, except occasionally to say how many babies were there at the time, which was approximately ninety, and how "frail and poorly" so many of them appeared to be. Mom mentioned seeing Mrs. Young during her visit. Although set on having a girl, Mrs. Young thought that mom and dad should have a good look at all of the babies before they made up their mind. As mom walked through the nursery and came to my crib, she bent down to have a better look, and that is when I got her! She was wearing a locket that dangled over me. I reached out, grasped the locket, and held on for dear life. It was apparent that the only way my mother was going home wearing her locket was to take me, a very determined child, dangling on the end of it.

I don't remember a time that I didn't know that I was adopted. It was certainly never a secret that I came from the Ideal Maternity Home, and was never an issue growing up in our home. Everyone knew about "Ruby's Boy," as I was often called. There was nothing to hide.

I was born Franklin Thomas Rutherford, and although my parents named me Larry Horton, they never officially changed my name. As I grew older it became increasingly clear that my mother was truly afraid I might find my birth parents. Because of this, I learned not to talk about that possibility, even though I at first secretly, then seriously, hoped that I could find them.

It was not until the last six to eight years that I began to seriously search for my birth family. It is not an easy decision to make and an even more difficult task to complete. As all too many adoptees discover when they embark on this journey, information is extremely difficult to come by.

My mother thought that my birth father, Robert Rutherford, had been in the military and was stationed at HMCS Stadaconna in Halifax during the war (at least at the time of my birth). I went to the Maritime Command Museum, on the base, to make some inquiries, and confirmed that a Robert Rutherford certainly had been there, attached to the base hospital. Unfortunately, they did not have a record of his service number. I could not understand why I was not born at the base hospital, since, when I did find my birth register, my mother was registered as Mrs. Robert Rutherford.

I then went to the Halifax Infirmary—the hospital where, apparently, I was born. Like many of the babies adopted from the Ideal Maternity Home, I was not born at the Home. At the Infirmary, I learned that all the birth records prior to 1960 had been destroyed. I don't remember making a scene, but my disappointment was evident enough to attract the attention of a staff person, who told me that the hospital still had the Delivery Room Register. There I found the entry that answered the questions that had plagued me for so long: May 24, 1943, Mrs. Robert Rutherford—twin boys. There was no time of birth or attending physician noted. Now a new set of questions surfaced. What happened to my twin brother? Did he die? Where is he now? How do I find him?

I contacted the Department of Children's and Family Services and eventually received a letter telling me that William Douglas Rutherford, my twin brother, had died, according to their records, on August 9, 1943, and was buried in the Fox Point Cemetery with a marker placed on his grave.

It was another two years before I could go to Fox Point to check out this information. When I visited the cemetery, there was no marker, or any record of his burial in any of the three cemeteries in Fox Point. Before leaving Nova Scotia that summer, I went to the Department of Vital Statistics, who produced my brother's death certificate.

As was indicated in *Butterbox Babies*, many of the official documents issued by the Ideal Maternity Home are not worth the paper they were written on. One glance at the death certificate for William Douglas Rutherford shows that half of the information was probably fabricated. Dr. Lila Young is listed as the attending physician verifying death, and as the official at burial. The signature itself should have elicited some question at the time of death. Lila Young wasn't a doctor, she was a midwife.

It was reported that many of the babies who died at the Ideal Maternity Home were buried in the vacant, now overgrown area adjacent to the Seventh Day Adventist Cemetery in Fox Point. Could my brother be buried there? Shouldn't there be some way to determine this? Did he even die as reported by the Youngs? How can I ever find the answers?

I am convinced that my brother is still alive. I often have feelings that are unrelated to any one in my adoptive family. My wife and I have come to believe that they resonate with my twin brother.

I have learned that in recent years, several babies who were supposed to have died in infancy have been found alive and have been reunited with their birth families. Considering the lack of evidence relating to my brother's death, I believe that he is alive and well. He may not even be aware of his birth circumstances.

Children and Family Services in Halifax have a last-known address for Mrs. Robert Rutherford in Winnipeg. That address no longer exists. When I applied for my long-form birth certificate, as part of an application for a visa to the Untied States, my father's birth place was listed as Ontario, with no date or specific location. I am searching for Robert Rutherford and Mary Ellen Stewart. Because a piece of information included in my application to the Public Archives did not match their records, they would not open my parents' file. I sent them an amended application, but to date have had no response.

In the meantime, I have some very good memories. My mom and dad were simple, God-fearing folk who loved me and provided my basic needs. My father was overjoyed with my choice to become a Christian minister, and my mother supported me in every way, on limited resources. We had our differences, but who hasn't? I am proud of my family—strong, stubborn, Scottish stock!

Over these past years, people have commonly asked me two questions: "Aren't you angry at your parents?" and, "Wouldn't you like to meet your real parents?" The answers are simple. I have no idea why I ended up at the Ideal Maternity Home. Those were perilous and uncertain times. Any number of circumstances could have applied. I simply trust that my birth parents did what they thought best for me at the time. I cannot imagine the anguish one might feel relinquishing your own flesh and blood. How could anyone be angry at their trying to do the right thing? Wouldn't I like to meet my real parents? I already know my real parents. I enjoyed them, until their recent passing. My birth parents gave me a body, but mom and dad gave me life, and the direction that brought me to the ministry. This direction has helped me immensely in my family life, which includes a wife, and three grown children who are now living on their own.

Would I like to meet my birth parents and siblings, if any? Yes! It would mean a great deal to me, but not at their expense and pain. Reunions, as many of the Survivors have discovered, are not always the joyous occasions envisioned and hoped for. I would especially love to meet my twin brother—I am sure he is alive.

I live with the hope that, one day, one of the many Rutherfords that I have contacted, or even someone out of the blue, will lay claim to me. Somewhere out there is a Rutherford who is connected to, or knows, the Robert Rutherford/Mary Ellen Stewart family. I sincerely believe that I am not alone in this family, or in this world.

I Treasure Their Love

R U S S E L L   C R O F T

R ussell Croft grew up close to the Ideal Maternity Home, where he was born in December 1934. His mother, Dorothy, who lived near Chester, met Lila Young at a church function, and they talked about the babies at the Home. Dorothy must have expressed more than a passing interest in adopting a child, because shortly after their conversation, Dr. and Mrs. Young arrived at her home with two young boys.

One was a healthy and happy redhead, and the other was Russell, a somewhat sickly four-month-old. When asked to make a choice, his sister, who was five years old at the time, and a redhead herself, took immediately to the redhead baby. Russell was thankful that his mother said, "No, I think we will take this sick baby as he needs a lot of love to help him." With that, the choice was made and Russell became a part of Dorothy's family. Making the choice was the easy part. His father, Carl, was at work, and his mother, in her enthusiasm, had neglected to wait until she could discuss her decision with him. The new little bundle of joy joined the family in his absence.

When he arrived home from work, Carl was led into the bedroom with hushed whispers to see a tiny baby sleeping comfortably in a dresser drawer. His mother was happy and excited, but his father was in shock. Carl didn't sleep all night for worrying about how he was going to manage with this new and sickly baby. This was the Depression, and times were hard. In the morning, he awoke to sounds of laughter coming from the kitchen, where he found his wife, daughter, and his parents, all gathered around the table, watching the tiny frail child having a bath. Then and there, he knew he would do whatever was necessary to help this little boy who had brought so much happiness to his family. Russell still has the little tub that was used for his first bath with his new family.

It was clear that he was not a well child. His grandfather suggested that his back and limbs be rubbed with olive oil, which his parents did for weeks. Good nutritious food replaced the diet of molasses and water that he received while at the Home. His sister recalls that he couldn't do much of anything that a four-month-old baby should have been able to do. He couldn't even lift his head, let alone roll over. He must have lacked stimulation, because he would only look at his hands. But with the love and care that he was given, he finally started to grow. During all this time, his father had nightmares that someone would come and take his new son away from them.

Russell (2 years old) and sister, Frances (1936).

In February 1942, Russell was legally adopted, before his father went overseas to war. He didn't know that he was adopted while he was growing up. It was a subject that was never discussed with him.

It wasn't until years later that he discovered the truth about his adoption. He had been living in Ontario, and in 1963 returned to Nova Scotia with his then wife. About a year later, his wife told him that she had been talking to a woman who referred to Russell as

Russell (August 1995).

"the adopted Croft boy." He didn't mention the conversation to his parents, but decided to ask them for his birth certificate. They began the process of obtaining it, but it wasn't until 1975 that one was finally issued.

Although he had no reason or desire to find his birth parents, his doctor suggested it would be good to have his family records for health reasons. To date, he is fairly healthy and says that if he does get sick, they will have to look for a cause, rather than assume it is family related. Russell is very thankful that he was taken into his loving and caring family. He treasures their love always. For Russell, saying "I was a survivor" is an understatement.

I Chose My Parents

Wade was born as Kevin Merle Langille, on February 1, 1943, and remained at the Ideal Maternity Home for almost two years until he was adopted. His parents, who lived in the LaHave Islands in Lunenburg County, travelled to East Chester by taxi with the intention of adopting a baby girl. Wade, like so many babies at the Home, changed their minds and "chose" his future parents.

When his parents arrived at the Home on January 12, 1945, they were greeted by Dr. Young, who told them that his wife, Lila, was ill, and took them to the front office where they filled out adoption papers. Their next stop was another room, where eight little boys, including Wade, were playing. His mother remembers that all eight boys had colds and one had rickets. The girl who was looking after the children had a long stick, and Wade's mother wondered what it was being used for. As Wade's parents entered the room, all eight of the boys ran toward them, but Wade got there first and held on to the woman who would become his mother before the day ended.

Dr. Young explained that there were another eighty-five children available for adoption and proceeded to take Wade's parents through the nurseries. As his mother left to follow Dr. Young, she could hear Wade screaming after her. They went to the sun-porch where there were fourteen cribs in a row, all with small babies in them, but Wade's mother could still hear him crying in the other room, and decided not to look at any other babies. Wade had found his family.

As he grew up, Wade was aware of being an adopted child from an early age, and always knew who his birth mother was, and where to find her. Even so, he never had the desire to look for her, as he was happy with his adoptive parents.

Wade and his dad, the day after "Coming Home"—January 13, 1945.

Wade at 4 years old.

Ol oReason to Come home

HOWARD COOPER

J was born George Glenwood Sweeney on June 3, 1946, at the Ideal Maternity Home in East Chester, Nova Scotia. Because the authorities were investigating the Youngs at that time, at only six days of age I was taken by a couple from Brooklyn, New York. Florence and Seymour Newman were unable to have children of their own so Seymour's father arranged that the necessary money be paid to the Youngs for a baby from the Ideal Maternity Home. Records revealed many years later that I was brought into the United States via Colonial Air Lines at Burlington, Vermont on June 9, 1946. The date of the Certificate of Arrival was July 25, 1951, more than five years after I was born.

When I arrived in the United States, my adopted parents changed my name to Howard Newman. I spent the first year or two of my life living in Parkchester—a section of the Bronx in New York City. Later, my family moved to Valley Stream, Long Island, where we lived until I was about six years old. We then moved to a small suburb of New York City called Woodmere, where we lived until I was thirteen.

As a child, I had a loving family, and my grandparents, who lived in Brooklyn, visited often. I was raised in a conservative Jewish home and was brought up with strong moral values. My adoptive father, Seymour, was a salesman for Philco and was on the road a lot in the New York City area. He spent the weekends with me, when we would often played ball, and he would umpire little league baseball games. I was very close to my father and also loved my mother, who spoiled me, as many Jewish mothers do to their children.

One day, when I was about five years old, I remember being taken to a large building in the city. The building had large columns and seemed important, but at five years old, I didn't really know what was going on. I later found out that this was the day that I was officially naturalized as a US citizen. The official records show that I was adopted on March 15, 1949, in the Bronx, that I was Canadian, and that my real name was George Glenwood Sweeney.

Although I was brought up in the Jewish tradition, I felt more like the kids in the neighbourhood who were not Jewish. Friends would often tell my mother that I looked like her and had her features. She would pretend that I was her natural son, and never mentioned that I was adopted. She did make a few vague remarks about picking me from a group of babies, but it did not really register with me until I entered high school and the clerk at the desk said to my mother, "Oh, he's adopted." Florence was shaken and asked if that mattered to me. I said it didn't make any difference to me, but later in life I would find out that it did.

One night in March 1958, I was awakened by my mother calling my father's name. She was saying, "Seymour, wake up, Seymour, wake up!" This continued for some time so I got out of bed and went into my parents' bedroom. My father was laying in bed, gasping for breath. When the ambulance arrived, my mother and I went into the den while the emergency people worked on my father. After a few minutes one of them came into the room and said, "He's gone." I was in shock. How could my father, who was strong and healthy just a few hours ago, be suddenly gone? This had a major impact on my life for many years. I continued to live with my mother as best I could, but had to have counselling because of problems I was having, both at home and at school.

A few years later, Florence married a wealthy man named Morris Cooper. He had a son in college and two daughters, one two years younger than me, as well as an older daughter who was also going into college. All of a sudden I went from being a lonely only child to having sisters and brothers. At first things went well, but Morris resented my close ties with my mother and often treated me badly. My new younger sister and I became very friendly and were shipped off to camp for the

Howard Cooper at the Waterfront, Brooklyn, NY (April 1949).

Howard and adoptive family at aunt and uncle's wedding—June 17, 1956.
(L-R) Howard, (mother) Florence, grandfather, aunt and uncle (bride and groom), grandmother, and father.

Howard and wife Mary join with Survivors for the special performance of Aftermath in New Jersey—April 1998.
(L-R) Howard, Sue Kuznet, and Mary.

Howard (1996).

summers so our parents could go off on trips to Europe and Asia.

Because of the bad relationship I had with my stepfather, I decided to go to Eastern Military Academy in Huntington, Long Island. I spent three years there in high school and did well enough to get into Ohio University in Athens, Ohio. College was an exciting time and I really enjoyed being on my own, but after two years, I had to leave because my grade point average fell below 2.0.

I worked in New York City, then returned to school, majoring in English and Secondary Education. At graduate school, I majored in Interpersonal Communication, because my best friend, Rudy, was working on his Ph.D. in Communication there. After getting my Master's degree in 1971, I moved out to California to be with Rudy, who was by then a professor at San Jose State University.

While working at the VA Medical Center in West Haven, I met a woman named Mary Smallman and fell in love. We got married on July 23, 1983, and a week later were on the road to Reno, Nevada, where I had taken a permanent job in Human Resource Management. Our son, Brendan, was born on November 12, 1985. It was the most exciting day of our lives. Mary stayed at home with Brendan during the next few months, and I had to learn to be a father, and to do things like change diapers and bathe my son.

It was about this time that Mary suggested I try to track down my real parents, so I contacted Ed Brownell at Parent Finders in Canada. I didn't know anything about my past, other than that I was born in Nova Scotia and that I was adopted. My mother told me that the place where I was born had burned down and that the records were destroyed. A short time later, I received a package from the State of New York concerning my citizenship, proof of which I had requested. The name George Glenwood Sweeney was on the Certificate of Arrival, which was dated June 12, 1946. "Who the heck is George Sweeney?" I wondered. Mary said that it must be my real name. The other papers showed that a baby by the name of George Sweeney was born in East Chester, Nova Scotia, and then became Howard Newman.

With this new information, Mr. Brownell was able to track down some Sweeneys in the Yarmouth area. When my birth mother Hilda heard that someone was asking questions, she knew what it was about. She phoned Mr. Brownell and told him that she had put a son up for adoption in 1946. When Mr. Brownell called me, my jaw just about hit the ground. I now had the number and name of my natural mother. I was very nervous, but made the call to Hilda, and was very relieved that she had always hoped her son would find her. It was very emotional and exciting. Hilda had always believed that some day her son would come knocking on her door, and so never moved from the Yarmouth area.

I flew to Nova Scotia to visit Hilda and meet the family. It was a very exiting time, and driving around Yarmouth was like taking a trip into history. Meeting so many family members was a very trying experience. I noticed a resemblance with many of the family, who all welcomed me like they had known me for years. Many of the men were fisherman and had lived hard lives. They were very basic people with strong family ties. I spent a few days in Yarmouth then flew back to Connecticut a new person.

When I got home, I had to tell everyone what happened and what it was like. I always enjoy visiting Mary's family because they make me feel at home and are more like my family than my adopted mother is. I could never really communicate with my adoptive mother, and was never able to share feelings with her like I could with Mary and her parents.

In 1989, following the death of her husband, Hilda visited us in Louisiana, and Mary and Brendan finally got to meet her. When she arrived, the local TV station had people at the airport to greet her, and the reunion was televised, then broadcast on Mother's Day.

In the summer of 1997, Mary, Brendan, and I flew to Maine and took the *Scotia Prince* over to Yarmouth. It was a great trip that we will never forget. When the ship approached the coast of Nova Scotia, a lighthouse was visible as we passed the small coastline with tiny houses and fishing boats lining the shore. Every place you gazed at looked like a painting. When the boat docked, Hilda met us and drove us to her house. She took us to the lighthouse and showed us all the Sweeney names on display inside the lighthouse, which is now a museum. All the people who worked there knew her family history on Cape Forchu.

One day we drove to Chester and toured the site of the infamous Ideal Maternity Home. It was very emotional for me to stand on the place of my birth, after many years of not knowing and searching.

To have my mother Hilda there with me was beyond words. We strolled around the grounds and had some photos taken, and were so pleased that we had this opportunity to be there together. We also had the opportunity to share our story with a reporter. When he asked about how Hilda felt about being back at the site of the Ideal Maternity Home, she smiled and said, "When I left here in 1946, I was glad to leave, but was worried about my baby. It sure feels good to come back here today, with him here beside me again."

Standing there with Mary, Brendan, and Hilda, I felt that I knew my history. I was back to my beginnings.

This is but one of the stories of the many babies born at the Ideal Maternity Home. I was very lucky that I was a healthy baby, and I was also lucky that I had good parents who loved me. They put me through college. I hate to think what might have happened to me if my adoptive parents hadn't come along when they did. I am also fortunate to have found my birth mother.

I consider myself lucky to have my life story now complete. I hope others will be able to be reunite with their families, get to know who they really are, and experience that personal closure in their lives.

See Hilda's story, "Memories of a Birth Mother," on page 19.

A New Family
—a New Identity

DAVID WILLIAM VOSBURGH

J was born at the Ideal Maternity Home on May 18, 1944, as Rex Albert McBride. As a child, I was raised with my older sister, Helen, in Elizabeth, New Jersey, by our parents, Ruth and Harry Vosburgh. Our family life was not exactly congenial. I rarely saw my father, and we never established a close relationship. My mother was very religious, but extremist in her views. When my sister and I inquired as to why we were both born in Nova Scotia (the perfect opportunity to disclose our adoptions), my mother vehemently denied there was any reason other than a medical necessity for her to see a specialist one thousand miles from home. I am somewhat bitter about her lies. Although both my sister and I were aware that we had been born in Canada, we did not question the circumstances, for our mother staunchly maintained that we were her natural children. Doubts again entered my mind when I became a naturalized citizen at the age of ten, but my mother refused to discuss it. As I got older, I acquiesced that since my birth certificate stated I was David William Vosburgh, that's who I must be.

I was neither encouraged nor provided with the means to attend college, although I had wanted to. I was not allowed to join groups or clubs other than church groups. I married my high school sweetheart, Dottie, at the age of twenty-one, and we moved to the Jersey Shore, where we raised three children of our own—two sons and a daughter. Even after Dottie and I were married, my parents rarely visited us. My father came to our home for one visit over a twenty-year period. I have worked for the Nestlé Company for thirty-two years, and became a superintendent there in 1971. I coached my sons' soccer teams and was an assistant boy scout leader, with my son attaining the rank of Eagle Scout. I'm a proud dad. All three of my children graduated from university with honours. My youngest son, Dale, was a National Merit Scholar when he graduated from high school five years ago (one of only two thousand in the United States) and is now a chemical engineer. My daughter, Diana, was named "Most Caring Senior" out of five hundred seniors in her high school class. She graduated *Magna Cum Laude* from university and now teaches deaf and hearing-impaired pre-schoolers. My oldest son, David, is a civil engineer. So although I was never lauded for my accomplishments, I have taken great pride in those of my children. I couldn't have been half as bad as my parents made me out to be!

On May 18, 1993, I celebrated my forty-ninth birthday as David William Vosburgh, the only identity I had ever known. Then, one fateful day during the summer of 1993, Dottie and I were vacationing in Nova Scotia. Looking for the hospital where I was born, we asked the proprietor of the East Chester Bed & Breakfast, Mr. Ross Davis, where the East Chester Hospital was located. He said that East Chester had no hospital and, over the next several hours, explained the story of the Ideal Maternity Home. I had driven right onto the property where I had been born! Needless to say, I was in shock. We immediately bought a copy of *Butterbox Babies*, and I could neither comprehend the ramifications of what I had just discovered about my origins nor deny being a part of the distressing drama. I was very concerned about how I was going to break the news to my sister Helen. When I telephoned her, I learned that she and her husband had visited Nova Scotia the previous week and discovered the truth before I had. She had been in a quandary over how to relay the news to me! The remainder of our vacation was spent trying to gather information on the Home, and on my birth identification, while also coming to terms with the idea of being adopted.

I read about a group of Survivors in *The Search*, and contacted Michael Reider, who helped me contact appropriate government agencies. Over a year later, I received a copy of the Petition for Naturalization my parents had filled out when I became a U.S. citizen. There before my eyes was my name at birth—Rex Albert McBride. I had entered the country on October 17, 1944, when I was five months old. My adoption had been finalized in New Brunswick, Canada. We then contacted Post-Adoption Services in New Brunswick, who instigated a search on my behalf. According to records on file, my adoption was finalized on October 4, 1944, in Saint John. I was put at the forefront of adoptee searches due to a medical condition, but it proved to be fruitless. I was informed that they had located a woman with my mother's name, but she denied our relationship. In September 1995, I requested a copy of my Order for Adoption, which I discovered I was entitled to under New Brunswick law. They complied, after obliterating all identifying information about my birth mother. Another dead end. I heard nothing further until January 1997, when Post-Adoption called to confirm that the woman they had initially contacted two years ago was, in fact, my mother. She had been unwilling at that time to acknowledge me as her son. Unfortunately, she had passed away on August 1, 1996, at the age of ninety-one in a nursing home in Ontario. I was informed that since there was a living sister who chose not to get involved because she knew nothing of my birth, I was still not entitled to any identifying identification. I was frustrated that even upon her death I could not learn my mother's identity, and sad that I had missed the opportunity to meet her. I composed a letter imploring her sister to reconsider, and sent it to her in care of Post-Adoption Services. To my surprise, she responded with a lengthy and informative letter detailing my family history. It was then that I learned my mother's name was Mary Evelyn Catherine McBride. I finally met my aunt, my uncle, and my cousin and his family in June 1997 in Ontario. They welcomed me warmly, and I felt as though I had known them all my life.

I received another shock when Post-Adoption Services called to inform me that I had a brother! It seems that a man nearing retirement had contacted them to obtain a copy of his birth certificate because he had been raised by a family after being in an orphanage. He had never been legally adopted and his birth mother's name was the same as mine. He informed Post-Adoption Services that he would like to be in contact

David's (Rex Albert McBride) passport photo, October 1944.

David and his sister (Helen), also adopted from the Ideal Maternity Home.

David's birth mother, Mary Evelyn McBride.

David, right, and his half brother Jim Lowe (both sons of Mary McBride).

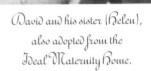

David and his sister Helen pose with Bette Cahill (centre), author of Butterbox Babies, at the August 30, 1997 performance of Aftermath.

with me, so I sent off another letter. Our reunion took place in August 1997 in New Brunswick, Canada. Again it was a homecoming of hearts. His nickname for me is "Kid," since I am fifteen years his junior.

Quite by accident, while vacationing in Nova Scotia that same summer, I stopped to ask directions in Digby. I saw a door ajar and went to inquire about the location of St. Anne's Parish to obtain genealogical information. The residents asked what name we were researching, and as "McBride" left my lips, a gasp of surprise left theirs. There I was, somehow led to the door of my second cousin, Graham, who I never even knew existed!

As I approach my 54th birthday, I feel blessed to have my wonderful sister, Helen (Claudia Ann Murphy), who has shared my life, as well as this incredible legacy of our past. Now I also have a brother Jim, an Aunt Eileen, an Uncle Bill, cousins Kevin and Carol-Jane, and a second cousin Graham. I never dreamed when I set out to visit Nova Scotia that my journey would lead me to a new family and identity! I thank everyone who has helped me in my search and made my happy ending possible.

But endings have a funny way of begetting beginnings. Just yesterday, April 22, 1998, I received a copy of my long sought after birth registration in the name of Rex Albert McBride. Attached to it was the Application for Immigration Visa filed on my behalf by my adoptive mother. And there, for the first time was a written record of my father's name, Mr. Rex Trusselle, R.C.A.F. And so, my search begins anew.

Forward and Back to My History

LEONARD GLICK

ecently, I found out something that most people take for granted: who they are and where they came from. I have no pictures of myself as an infant; none of those "in the hospital photos" of a scrunched up red-faced baby about whom everyone says, "Oh how beautiful," when they really want to say, "Things can only get better."

I don't know why my adoptive parents didn't tell me I was adopted. Were they afraid I would not love them, or that I would run off to find my biological parents? All of these fears, for them, were real. Who can say they were wrong?

I was born in East Chester, Nova Scotia, on May 4, 1944, and I was adopted from a place called the Ideal Maternity Home in February 1946, by Harry and Marcelle Glick of Bronx, NY. Harry and Marcelle had a son of their own, who had died at age twenty-one, six weeks before I was born. They were devastated, and I don't think they ever recovered. Marcelle wanted another child desperately; Harry was against it.

They were precisely the kind of client the Ideal Maternity Home was looking for. They were too old to adopt a child legally in the United States, and they were Jewish, which meant that they were only permitted to adopt a child born of Jewish parents—and there were no Jewish babies up for adoption at that time. They were also well-to-do, which meant they could buy a baby from the Home. Money was the name of the game at the Ideal Maternity Home, and religion was not of primary concern to the Youngs—they would fabricate the religion of the birth parents if necessary.

They brought me to the United States in 1946, and we lived in New York until 1957. We were "Snowbirds"—six months in New York, six months in Miami Beach, Florida. I had a wonderful childhood. Harry and Marcelle were the best parents anyone could ask for. I was the miracle child that gave them a reason to go on. No child could have been more loved, and nothing that has happened will ever diminish my love for them or minimize what they did for me.

I never had any reason to doubt that they were my real parents. They said I was born in Nova Scotia while they were on a sport fishing vacation. It was true that Harry went to Wedgeport, Nova Scotia, each year with friends to fish for giant tuna. The story didn't seem so far-fetched.

I remember going to the Federal Courthouse in New York to become a naturalized citizen in 1954. I was told that this was necessary, since I had been born in Canada. No one (friends, relatives, etc.) broke the vow of secrecy Marcelle had sworn them to. It was not until I met my wife, Dianne, in 1962, that I began to doubt my history. Most men, myself included, are not very perceptive.

Dianne immediately doubted the story, and for good reasons: her parents and their friends were much younger than mine; there were no baby pictures of me; and Marcelle Glick, in her late 40s and nine months pregnant, going to rural Nova Scotia, with who knows what type of medical facilities available, to fish for tuna? Not a chance. This, coupled with the loss of Marcelle's only child one year before, made the story all the more suspect.

The clincher for Dianne though was the naturalization issue. She reasoned that if Marcelle was a U.S. citizen, I could have been born on the moon and would be one too.

In 1968, I requested a copy of my birth certificate from the registrar in Nova Scotia. Six weeks later, I received an official document. It detailed my place of birth, my date of birth, and the name of my birth mother. You guessed it! It was not Marcelle Glick; it was Cora Glidden. There was a blank space where the name of the father should have been.

My name was listed as Leonard Wayne Glidden. At the bottom of the form were the details of the adoption proceeding.

This did not come as a total surprise. But I wasn't going to rush off in a frenzied search for a mother I never knew. I never told my parents; to the day they passed away in 1976, and 1986, their secret was safe with me.

At the end of the summer, I drove to East Chester, Nova Scotia, as a tourist. Since I knew the name of the town I was born in, I thought I should visit the area. I struck up a conversation with one of the local merchants and explained that I was born in East Chester, adopted, and taken to New York. He said I was probably born at "Dr. Young's foundling home ... a lot of Americans got kids from there." He directed me to what were the remains of a building in an empty field. I looked, and I left.

In 1996, my judicial assistant, Pat Compton, travelled to Halifax, Nova Scotia, and, knowing my "history," went to Chester and asked the woman who ran the local bed and breakfast about the Ideal Maternity Home. The woman told her the story of the Home and referred her to the book *Butterbox Babies*.

When Pat went to a book store in Halifax to buy the book, another shopper noticed the purchase and said she knew the author and gave her Betty Cahill's number.

I called Betty, and she put me in touch with Bob Hartlen in Nova Scotia, who heads up the Survivors and Friends of the Ideal Maternity Home.

Dianne and I decided to go to the reunion of the Survivors planned for the end of August 1997. Prior to going, I wrote to the registrar in Halifax asking for a copy of my birth certificate. I was hoping against hope that they would send a duplicate of the one I received in 1968. I was wrong.

The laws had changed, and certificates like that were now unobtainable. Instead, they send you a registration of birth with the names of the adoptive parents listed as the birth parents. In all matters of adoption, even as an adult, you are denied access to your history.

By separate letter, the registrar did send what they called "non-identifying" data about the woman their records showed as my birth mother. At the time of my birth she was twenty-one and lived in the Halifax area. She was born in Gravenhurst, Ontario, of Irish parents. I was her second child.

We had a wonderful time at the reunion, met lovely people, and shared information. We met Mike Slayter and Faith Hendrickson of Parent

Finders Nova Scotia, and agreed to have them start a search for Cora Glidden.

On November 4, 1997, Faith and Mike called to say, "We think we found your mother."

Coincidentally, when they were researching the name Glidden at the library in Gravenhurst, the librarian they spoke to turned out to be my cousin.

I called the librarian and levelled with her. I told her who I was and explained that I did not want to intrude on anyone's life but I needed to know if her Aunt Cora was my birth mother. She asked me to call back in fifteen minutes. When I called back, she told me she had spoken with her Aunt Cora, and that she wanted to know more about my circumstances. At that moment, I knew that I had the right Cora Glidden.

When I finally got up the nerve to call Cora, she said in her clipped, no-nonsense way of speaking, "Tell me more about yourself." "My name as I remember it from my birth certificate is Leonard Wayne Glidden," I began.

She stopped me cold. "You don't have to go any further," she said "I'm your mother!"

It was all uphill from there. Over the next hour on the phone (it seemed like five minutes), I learned about the woman who gave birth to me at the Ideal Maternity Home, and who had no choice but to give me up for adoption so I might have the chance for a better life. She had no money, no husband, no possibility of giving me the things one would want for their child. She had no options. Before leaving the maternity home, she had second thoughts. She tried to get me back, but they told her I was dead, and she had no reason not to believe them; my birth had been a difficult one.

On November 10, one week after the search began, I was reunited with my mother in Winnipeg. She could not wait. She met me in the lobby of her apartment building, and there was no getting away from it—we do look alike.

We spent the next two days getting acquainted. It was very easy; almost like visiting an aunt you haven't seen for a while and catching up on family stuff.

It was not only a happy ending to my search, it was a happy beginning to the next chapter in all our lives.

See Cora's story, "A Second Chance," on page 13.

Cora Glidden— Leonard's birth mother (approx. 1944).

Leonard Glick (approx. 2–3 years old).

Leonard at 7 years old.

Judge Leonard Glick—1996.

Leonard reunited with mother, Cora (Glidden) Kennedy, in Winnipeg, Manitoba, November 1997.

The Search Begins

MICHAEL REIDER

ichael Reider was born Louis Lawrence MacKenzie on January 21, 1945. He was adopted when he was sixteen months old by a Jewish family from New Jersey, where he grew up. Michael didn't begin searching for his birth family until after his marriage in 1985. When his wife, Norma, heard the story of his adoption, she felt something wasn't quite right about it. At her suggestion, Michael sent for his Nova Scotia birth certificate, using his birth name. He felt that if he received an answer, he would know the adoption wasn't legal, in Canada at least. Imagine their surprise when it actually arrived in the mail a few weeks later.

Following this, his adopted mom sent him a New Jersey document listing the names of Mike's parents. His father's name was Louis MacKenzie. This didn't make sense to him. Why would a mother give her baby the father's name if she had intended to give him away? At the very least, it might be assumed that his parents loved each other.

For the next two years, Norma called people on the east coast and explained who she was and what she was calling about. Everyone she spoke with was sympathetic, but not helpful. She spoke with three women with the same name as Mike's mother. One of them was a nun, and a little upset that her own brother had given them her phone number, and no, she assured them, she was not Michael's mother. So, they decided to look for Michael's father. Michael wrote to the government, requesting information about where his father was buried, on the pretext he had died in the war. There was nothing to indicate that his father had ever served in the war. Meanwhile, they continued to make calls, without success. One night, Norma decided to make just a few more calls, and started on a list from the phone book. As she started to dial a number on the list, Michael said it was useless, as the name was spelled Mc instead of Mac. Norma persisted, saying, "Just this one call." A woman answered the phone and Norma asked for D. McKenzie (the listing in the book) and was told that he was not there. She said that she was actually looking for Louis McKenzie. "Oh, that would be D's father," the woman replied. Norma explained who she was and why she was calling, and asked the woman if she was familiar with the Butterbox Baby story. "More than you know," was the response. Norma told her Michael's birth date, and the woman began asking a barrage of questions: "Where do you live?" "What does Michael do for a living?" "How many children do you have?" Finally, Norma asked, "Are you a relative of my husband's?" "Yes," was the hushed reply. They had found Michael's mother!

Michael age 8/9 years.

It took several months for Michael's mother to talk with him. She was afraid he would hate her and he was afraid that she would reject him. Finally, after many phone conversations, Norma insisted that they were both being ridiculous and literally thrust the phone at Michael. They finally had that first conversation, on eggshells, but both were relieved afterwards that it had gone well.

She said that when she had Michael, his father was overseas and she went to the Home due to the financial situation at home. Her husband told her to leave Michael there and they would bring him home when he returned. She left him, paying room and board for a year. After Louis came home in 1946, they went to the Home for him, but Lila told them that Michael had been adopted by a couple in the United States, and that if they really wanted him back, they would have to pay $12,000.

As his mother said, even the family farm wasn't worth that much, and they had no choice but to go home without him.

Unknown to them, Michael, who was thirteen months old at this time, was still at the Home, and remained there until he was sixteen months old, when he was adopted by the Reiders.

Michael's birth parents went on to have eight more children; five girls and three boys. The children were never told about their older brother, as the guilt over leaving him never left his mother. She blamed her husband for years, making their lives quite difficult at times. When she told Mike and Norma the whole story, and how she felt about what she had seen at the Home, and what hell it had been ever since, wondering where Michael was, it was the first time that she had told anyone in over forty years. She could feel the weight lifted off her shoulders and in its place a sense of peace like she had never known.

On November 11, 1988, the Canadian Broadcasting Corporation (CBC) aired what would be the first of many stories about the Ideal Maternity Home. In a series of interviews with other Survivors of the Home, Michael and his adoptive mother, Florence, spoke of some of the circumstances surrounding Michael's adoption. Michael said that his parents paid $10,000 to adopt him, and even after paying this, they were asked to make another cash contribution to the Ideal Maternity Home, which they refused to pay.

Mrs. Reider recalled picking Michael from an unruly pack of babies at the Home. During the interview she said, "They were wild, running around, screaming, no discipline, and no one taking care of them; they were just doing what they wanted to do." She said of Michael, "As I walked past his crib with my friend, I said, 'Isn't he adorable?' I had no regrets dealing with the Home. I felt they gave me what I wanted. I've been happy with Michael all my life and very happy with the way he turned out."

Michael's birth mother and one of his sisters visited him in Ontario for a weekend. It was his mother's first ever plane trip. Mike and Norma met them at the airport, examining every older woman travelling with a younger one, saying to each other, "How about that one?" Finally, they saw them on the escalator and knew at once who they were. As they were saying, "There they are," the women were doing the same back. It was the most bizarre, wonderful weekend—one that they will never forget. Michael not only looks like his mother, but even his personality resembles hers.

The following summer, Michael and Norma went to visit the whole family on the east coast. Some of Mike's brothers and sisters weren't told about him until twenty-four hours before meeting him. The whole thing was very exhausting, exhilarating, and wonderful. They went on bus tours, had wonderful dinners, looked through the family albums, and Michael's dad told him all about the war. They welcomed Mike, Norma, and their two children into their family.

Michael (grade 12).

Since reuniting with his birth family a few years ago, Michael has developed close friendships with several of his five sisters and three brothers. Though his birth father passed away soon after being found by Michael and Norma, it will always be a happy memory that they were able to meet several times.

Michael's birth mother now lives with one of his sisters away from the family farm. Florence, his adoptive mother, an energetic ninety-six-year old, lives in a senior's home nearby Michael's hometown of Woodville, Ontario.

Norma, who has been at Mike's right hand throughout his search and reunion, participated in the first memorial service for the Butterbox Babies who died at the Home. Being an accomplished

Michael (1997).

pianist, she composed many pieces of music over a period of years that were inspired by their personal search and the unfolding story of the Butterbox Babies. One piece of music in particular, entitled "Where Have You Gone?" for which she also wrote lyrics, was played at the first memorial service. This beautiful piece of music, with its haunting melody, was also performed in 1987 in the play *Aftermath*, in addition to being sung at the second memorial service.

Where Have You Gone?
It happened in Nova Scotia, where a girl had a lover so dear.
But he sailed on a ship and he went to the war,
That he'd never return was her fear.
But a child was growing within her, and she carried the secret alone,
Crying out to the one who had left her behind,
Lover where are you, where have you gone?
So she went to a home in Lunenburg, where in peace she could hide her
*   shame*
And her golden-haired girl could be born to the world, without the fear
*   and the blame.*
And they told her to leave her little one for someone else to raise,
But for years her heart ached and she heard her girl cry,
"Momma where are you, where have you gone?"
They say some of them went to New Jersey, and that all are hard to find,
And that some were merely forgotten in time
They're the ones who were left behind.
Well I have my own child before me, and he's safe in my arms as can be,
And I'll teach him to ask what's important to know,
Where are the children, where have they gone?
The shades are down, and he's dreaming, but the shadows aren't hard to
*   find,*
Cause I have this feeling of sorrow inside, for the ones that were left behind
O, where is the girl with the golden hair, and the boy with the eyes so blue,
And the one who can't hear his mother's cry
"Baby where are you, where have you gone?"

Norma Reider

APPENDICES

To Overcome
the Barriers to Identity

APPENDIX I

Mike Slayter is a spokesperson for Parent Finders Nova Scotia. He is also a member of the Adoption Council of Canada, and of the Ministerial Committee on Adoption Information Disclosure.

he story of the Ideal Maternity Home is indisputably filled with tragedy and loss. It is incomprehensible that events cloaked in deception and secrecy were allowed to occur in the first place. I was not born at the Home, although I was born in an era when social mores brought the wrath of a self-righteous and condemning society to bear harshly on pregnant, unmarried mothers. Children, born innocently outside of wedlock, had few of the potential benefits afforded to legitimate babies born into family homes, unless they were adopted into a two-parent home. For the babies born at the Home, their start in life, whether predetermined or not, was marred by the greed of the notorious owners of the Ideal Maternity Home, who turned illegitimate babies into a commodity. Throwing good intentions to the wind, Lila and William Young developed the business of selling illegitimate babies to adoptive homes. Although reportedly hundreds of babies did not survive infancy due to neglect and the inadequate facilities of the Ideal Maternity Home, many did survive, saved by childless couples who travelled from near and far to have a chance at building a family of their own.

Life can be difficult enough without furthering its challenge to inno-cent children. Despite its good intentions, adoption can be a traumatic experience. Many Survivors of the Home came to view their adoption in their later years with a sense of loss and bewilderment. I was not one of the Survivors, but I am an adoptee. Born in the mid-50s, I knew of my adoption from my early years. Like many Survivors, I grew up in a loving family, but with a feeling of incompleteness; in psychological language, "identity bewilderment."

As a result, many of us have undertaken a quest to find ourselves. Deprived of the fundamental knowledge of who we are, and caught up in a web of deception, we are unable to chart a course through life because many of the signposts are missing.

The Survivors of the Ideal Maternity Home represent a family in their own right. Their common experience has created a bond that is palpa-ble in the recounting of their stories here. I came to know about this special family in the mid-90s after meeting Bob Hartlen, the author of this book. Bob attended a monthly meeting of Parent Finders Nova Scotia, and shared his personal experience with the group, and also found out what the group could offer him in terms of support for his small but ever-increasing group of Survivors. Parent Finders already had a few members who were Survivors of the Ideal Maternity Home, and although it offered hope in finding birth family members, it could not offer the unique support and camaraderie of Bob's group.

Parent Finders Nova Scotia is one of many support groups across the country that were born from the need of those affected by adoption. Founded in the mid-70s by Ms. Joan Vanstone, an adoptee herself, and by other adoptees, Parent Finders originated in British Columbia, with chapters soon sprouting up all across the country. The success of Parent Finders is due largely to its lobbying efforts for access to vital informa-tion withheld through provincial legislation from the adoption com-munity, yet made available to everyone else. It also provides a network of assistance in reuniting members of the adoption triad with each other. Through sheer tenacity, Joan has developed the Canadian Adoption Reunion Registry (the largest in Canada), which presently boasts in excess of 45,000 names.

Unfortunately, entitlement to information does not always lead to the truth. In the case of the Ideal Maternity Home, stories were fabricated by the proprietors to cover their deceptions. For instance, birth mothers were told that their babies died when in fact they had not, information about a baby's biological background was invented to suit the wishes of adoptive parents, and identities both of birth mothers and of babies were changed to obscure the trail. Society's condemnation of unmarried mothers-to-be no doubt gave rise to professional secrecy and deception. These indiscretions, perpetrated by people like the Youngs, were ignored by the authorities—a consequence of the minimal laws governing adoption practice in those days. Although new legislation curbing the marketing of infants, and other unsavoury practices exercised by private agencies, was eventually passed, not much has changed with respect to accessing information about an adopted child's heritage and birth parentage.

More than fifty years after the forced closing of the Ideal Maternity Home by provincial social services, adoptees are still not entitled to identifying information about their birth families, and birth parents are still denied access to information about their children relinquished to adoption. The tragedy of the infant deaths at the Ideal Maternity Home cannot be reversed. But the tragedy of babies who were displaced from their communities and birth families continues with the perpetuation of sealed records.

Today, in this province, Parent Finders and the Survivors and Friends of the Ideal Maternity Home support each other in their lobbying efforts to locate birth families. For many born at the Ideal Maternity Home, time is running out for finding a connection of any kind to any member(s) of their birth families—siblings, half-siblings, cousins, and many other extended family members.

I have witnessed reunions that were never thought possible, accomplished with very little, if any, help from the government. Ironically, it is the government, specifically the Departments of Community Services and Vital Statistics, that withholds information that is key to making contact with the birth family. Because of restrictive disclosure legislation, the government will not provide copies of original long-form birth certificates to adoptees. This legislation is a holdover from the 1940s and 50s' practice of effectively sealing birth certificates in order to prevent adoptees from uncovering their roots. Despite the hearings of a special ministerial committee in 1994, the federal government remains unmoved. In 1975, England enacted legislation allowing adult adoptees entitlement to their original birth certificates; other countries throughout the world followed suit. Recently, British Columbia, through provincial legislation, enacted a new law entitling adoptees to procure a copy of their long-form birth certificate. This is a hopeful development, and we remain resolved to bring about changes to a discriminatory law that views, and treats, adoptees as second-class citizens.

It is an anomaly in such a free and supposedly progressive country as Canada—a country that professes rights and freedoms for all—that the adoption community must endure this continuing hypocrisy.

Parent Finders Nova Scotia

Reuniting Families Separated by Adoption and Fostering

APPENDIX II

*P*arent Finders Nova Scotia is a non-profit volunteer-based support group for all members of the adoption community. Parent Finders was started in Vancouver in 1975 by several adoptees, including Joan Vanstone, who wanted to know the truth about their biological background and heritage. Through Joan's work and dedication over the years, Parent Finders has extended nationally, with chapters in each province, as well as several in the United States. Parent Finders Nova Scotia, active since 1975 under the direction of such dedicated people as Ed Brownwell and Ann White, has over six hundred members.

The primary objective of Parent Finders is to seek the truth about adoptions, and to end the secrecy of closed adoption files. They believe that everyone has the right to know who they really are, and their place on the genealogical map of life.

Parent Finders Nova Scotia holds an open monthly meeting at the I.W.K Grace Hospital, University Avenue, Halifax, NS, at 1:30 P.M. on the second Sunday of each month. Topics discussed cover a wide spectrum, from emotions and feelings about being adopted, to the issues of relinquishment, guilt, and hurt associated with birth mothers. In short, we talk about being adopted and why we need to know the truth about our past so that we can make sense of the present and future; we assist our members in their search for their birth families by suggesting avenues of reference that may be available through the public libraries or Archives; we produce a quarterly newsletter entitled *The Open Record*, which is sent to each of our members, as well as to other chapters of Parent Finders across Canada; we continue to lobby the government on behalf of the adoption community for change to present disclosure legislation; and we continue to heighten awareness of our plight, so that everyone may understand the issues and consequences of such damaging social policies and government insensitivity.

Parent Finders Nova Scotia has a lifetime membership fee of $25, and a yearly renewal fee of $10 to cover the cost of the quarterly newsletter. Its executive team members are nominated and elected by the general membership. The executive is composed of two group leaders, a registrar, search team coordinator, treasurer, and fundraising chairperson. One of the two group leaders also fills the position of spokesperson for Parent Finders Nova Scotia.

For more information contact:
Parent Finders Nova Scotia
Box 791, Lower Sackville
Nova Scotia B4C 3V3
Telephone (902) 864-6654
or (902) 435-0287

"Digger from Hell"

APPENDIX III

Faith is a member of Parent Finders Nova Scotia. Although not a Survivor of the Ideal Maternity Home, Faith's life was also touched by adoption. In her personal search for her brother, she encountered closed doors and sealed records. Not only did she ultimately succeed in her personal search, but, since 1993, she has also successfully searched for and reunited more than eighty families separated by adoption.

My name is Faith. Some people refer to me as the "Digger from Hell." I joined the support group Parent Finders Nova Scotia in January 1993. With their support and help, I located my brother in New York State. It was a happy reunion. My brother, Gary, was forty-two years old when he came to Nova Scotia and embraced his birth mother and siblings for the very first time.

I decided to stay with Parent Finders, and help others to know the truth of their origins, or find their children, now adults, whom they had relinquished for adoption.

It was at Parent Finders' monthly meetings that I met Survivors of the infamous Ideal Maternity Home. Their stories touched my heart, and I wanted to help them search. I read the book, watched the movie, talked with elderly folk who had grown up through that era, and who had known the story of the Ideal Maternity Home.

Many Survivors had little knowledge about their past; some had only scant information, and others had none. A lucky few had their original birth names.

Searching for information about one's past is a roller-coaster of emotions, and quite often a financial struggle that may lead nowhere. Barriers of secrecy from adoptive parents, and brick walls put up by bureaucrats and social workers are the most hurtful frustrations. The privately run adoption agency of Lila and William Young supposedly took little information from birth parents, and what records there may have been, reportedly burned in a fire.

My search for truth and identity for the Survivors continues. One of these Survivors, Betty Caumartin, asked for my help in her search. She had searched on and off for thirty years. I took the little information she had, made three telephone calls, and located her birth family in a matter of two hours. Birth mothers of the 1930s and 40s were told to forget their babies, and to never think about having contact with their children again. Some of the birth mothers were told that their babies had died shortly after birth, thus resulting in a whole different search approach by the adult adoptee looking to make contact with their now elderly birth mothers.

In Betty's case, Parent Finders' Mike Slayter made a personal approach on her behalf. Any type of approach by one other than a birth family member is not Parent Finders' policy, but there are always exceptions. Mike made a very sensitive approach, assuring Betty's birth mother of discretion and understanding. Betty and her birth mother met for their first embrace in our living room downstairs while Mike and I stayed upstairs. The tears of joy were uncontrollable from both sides, and the need for knowledge of each other's lives took hours to unfold. Betty now feels like a whole person who knows her heritage.

I met Justice Leonard Glick during the August 1997 Survivors Reunion in Chester, Nova Scotia, when many people from the United States who had been born at the Ideal Maternity Home came home to Canada—their birth place. Justice Glick was one of them. I introduced myself and told him that if he ever decided to search for his birth parents, he could call me. After he returned to his home in Miami, Florida, Justice Glick called a CBS News station, and asked if they could possibly help. They were more than willing to assist him in his quest.

The station's news team contacted Parent Finders' spokesperson Mike Slayter to tell him that they were assisting Justice Glick, and that they would be flying to Halifax to film a news story about Justice Glick and the Ideal Maternity Home. They asked Mike if Parent Finders Nova Scotia could locate Justice Glick's birth mother before they arrived in Halifax—in three days time. Mike asked me to take up the challenge. I immediately phoned Justice Glick for his agreement, and he gave me his birth name and the name of the county where his mother was apparently born. My search began at 8:15 Tuesday evening and ended at 9:20 that same evening, and cost Justice Glick only $24.85, for the telephone calls. I had established, in that short space of time, that his birth mother was alive and living in Manitoba.

I have no access to government records, motor vehicle registration, police records or even medical insurance records. I have only the information given to me, my instincts, and my telephone.

Carrie Matheson is another Survivor I met at the August 1997 reunion. I gave her a contact name in New Brunswick and her search for truth was also successful, as was her reunion with her birth family.

Parent Finders' member and Ideal Maternity Home Survivor, Rose Neil had me help in her search too. Hers was an expensive search, as it led down many paths. I discovered where her birth mother had worked during the 1930s, and found out what she looked like, but Rose was unable to continue the search. Another Parent Finder searcher, Glenda, wrote to a friend on Rose's behalf. The friend was living in the community where Rose's birth mother had been born. The outcome of the letter resulted in Rose speaking to her birth mother for the first time in her life, in April 1998.

It is not an easy task to search for another's past. Their feelings and frustrations are constantly on my mind. The search may also be expensive if it is undertaken in several countries.

I do not charge a fee for my services, but once I get permission to search, I expect to be reimbursed for the calls I make. Most adult adoptees and Survivors of the Ideal Maternity Home will say: "Do whatever it takes to find my birth roots, my birth family. I just want the truth."

One ongoing search is for the birth mother of another Survivor, Bill Holmes. This search is particularly frustrating, as Bill's adoptive mother, who is now deceased, told him different stories about his birth name. Nova Scotia's Department of Community Services claim they have little information on file. Bill's search has cost him hundreds of dollars and hours of hurtful hopelessness. I have at least been able to verify who Bill's birth father is, although he died years ago. I was also able to verify the identity of Bill's half-sister, who had died at the age of forty-two, before Bill ever got to meet her. Bill has been reunited with one of his nieces and has talked to people who knew his birth father.

Bill Holmes is going blind and is very ill. Yet he is still denied his adoption file from Nova Scotia's Department of Community Services. I have pleaded his case many times, before various committees and politicians, but he still has no access to the information he so desperately needs.

Searching in the Public Archives, libraries, and through other sources, requires many hours of devoted volunteers' time. Each search is unique, yet all have a tragic but common thread: very little available information.

It is quite therapeutic both for adult adoptees and for birth parents to become involved in their own searches. No matter how small or meaningless a piece of information may seem, everything helps to fit all the pieces of the puzzle together. I believe the right to know outweighs the right to privacy. Parent Finders Nova Scotia continues to lobby for change in our adoption disclosure laws, but it will take the voices of a great many to bring about that change.

Survivors and Friends in Search

The following is a list of adoptees from the Ideal Maternity Home who are either searching for, or are being searched for by, their birth families. The reference numbers following the names should be used when making inquiries about individuals on this list.

Between 1925-1928: Baby Girl, Langille (no reference #)

Between 1939–1941: Baby Girl, Moore/Tracy (?) (#133)

Between 1944–1946: Naugler/Maynard (?), Barbara Ann (#70)

1933, July 6: Baby Girl (#59)

1934, Dec 4: Baby Boy (#101)

1935, May 18: Kipper, Dolly Anita Mae (#36)

1935, Nov 9: Brown, Kenneth Victor (#2)

1936, May 7: MacDonald, Kathleen Elizabeth Ann (?) (#131)

1936, Dec 4: MacDonald, Harlon (#102)

1937: Jenning, Rose Marie (#74)

1937, Jan 25: Farien, Baby Boy (#132)

1937, Apr 5: Baby Girl (#172)

1937, Jun 1: Kerr, Keir Murray (#44)

1937, Dec 30: Skerry, Patricia Ann (#89)

1937, Feb 23: Witt, Kathleen (#64)

1939, Mar 2: Downie, Frank (#35)

1939, Jun 19: Baker, Vernon Kenneth (#104)

1940, Jan 31: Flewelling, Loraine May (#120)

1940, Apr 18: Baby Girl (#176)

1940, July 7: Eisenhauer, Faith Lu (#3)

1940, Nov 19: Baby Boy (#112)

1941, ?: Summerhayes, Florence (#139)

1941, Jan 30: Rhodenizer, William Roy (no reference #)

1941, Feb 9: Arab, Ronald Anthony (#168)

1941, Mar 1: Lucus, Francis Vaughn (#5)

1941, Mar 2: McCully, Joan Frances (#105)

1941, Apr 23: Meisner, Lowell Keith (#134)

1941, May 24: Golden, Barbara Joan (#135)

1941, Jun 2: Church, Goldie June (#100)

1941, Aug 1: Baby Boy (#163)

1941, Sep 7: Sager, Keith Robert

1941, Oct 31: Fitzmaurice, Beverley (#58)

1941, Nov 7: Smith, Patricia (#178)

1941, Nov 9: Paynter, Lorraine (#66)

1941, Nov 27: Webb, Geraldine Rose (#6)

1941, Dec 9: Callbeck, Carl Ray (#141)

1942, Jan 16: Johnson, Joan Isabel (#7)

1942, Feb 26: Bain, Lila Ann (#65)

1942, Mar 5: England, Olga Lorraine (#12)

1942, Mar 6: Murphy, Claudia Ann

1942, Apr 14: Ridgeway, Jane Shelly (#113)

1942, Apr 16: Baby Girl (Bertha Pearl) (#13)

1942, Jun 29: Clark, David Lorne (#39)

1942, July 14: Gregory, Jerry Malcolm (#25)

1942, July 27: Baby Girl (#161)

1942, Sep 13: Baby Girl (#143)

1942, Sept 13: Baby Girl (#144)

1942, Oct 16: Baby Boy (#29)

1942, Oct 28: Branscombe, Richard Leslie (#125)

1942, Dec 5: Baby Girl (#155)

1942, Dec 13: Cook, Gladys Mae

1943, ?: Morris, James Douglas (#146)

1943, Feb 1: Langille, Kevin Merle (#166)

1943, Feb 6: Mounstephen, Robert Sterling (#15)

1943, Mar 19: Powers, Edward (#159)

1943, Apr 4: Little, Baby Boy (#173)

1943, May 24: Rutherford, Thomas (#137)

1943, May 24: Rutherford, William Douglas (#137A)

1943, Jun 16: Carr, Patricia Ann (#16)

1943, Aug 8: Atkinson, Daniel Irvin (#41)

1943, Sep 14: Baby Boy (#156)

1943, Sep 25: Baby Girl (#97)

1943, Nov 13: Boozan, Rene Frances (#17)

1943, Nov 25: Black, Joseph William (#153)

1943, Dec 25: Vere-Holloway, Fern Elizabeth (#18)

1944, Jan 29: Richard, Ann Marie (#33)

1944, Jan 30: MacIntosh, Patricia (#43)

1944, Feb 27: Baby Girl (#167)

1944, Apr 5: Baby Girl (#186)

1944, Apr 17: DeYoung, Terry Russell (#49)

1944, May 22: Cleaves, Deloras Louise (#157)

1944, July 24: Baby Girl (Robin) (#95)

1944, July 26: Boudreau, Margaret Ann (#140)

1944, Aug 15: Caron, Claude (#126)

1944, Sep 27: Carr, Samuel Maurice (#22)

1944, Dec 10: Langille, Mary Nancy (#30)

1944, Dec 31: Dugan, Leona (#121)

1945, Jan 12: Baby Boy (#38)

1945, Feb 12: Baby Girl (#107)

1945, Mar 19: Boulter, Dale Robert (#127)

1945, Mar 21: Austin, Donna Marie (#57)

1945, Mar 27: Driscoll, Angela Mary (#68)

1945, Mar 29: Barnett, Charles William (#23)

1945, Apr: Baby Girl (#147)

1945, Apr 22: June Colleen Kennedy (#8)

1945, Apr 22: Stella Elizabeth Kennedy (#8A)

1945, May 21: Robichaud, Harry Jay (#79)

1945, Jun 9: Baby Boy (#117)

1945, Jun 13: MacLaughlin, Harry Edward (#31)

1945, July: Polson, Baby Girl (#37)

1945, July 16: Kynock, Gloria Jean (#108)

1945, July 20: Baby Girl (#130)

1945, Aug 1: Silver, Baby Girl (#164)

1945, Aug 2: Silver, Maryanne (#165)

1945, Aug 3: White, William Jay (#73)

1945, Sep 1: Guy, Barbara (#91)

1945, Sep 9: Baby Girl (#118)

1945, Sep 29: McKinnon, Felicity (#151)

1945, Sep 30: Weinstein, Lynn Merle (#149)

1945, Nov 23: Newell, Roxy Ilene (#177)

1945, Nov 25: Hartling, David (#162)

1945, Nov 27: Hopper, Wendy (#128)

1945, Dec 1: Hoddinot, Rayburn (#171)

1946, Jan 7: Baby Girl (#148)

1946, Jan 31: Longmire, Jo Ann Linda (#63)

1946, Feb 25: Baby Boy (#85)

1946, Mar 3: Amon, Robert Earl (#124)

1946, Mar 29: Stewart, Douglas James (#152)

1946, Apr 11: Baby Boy (#69)

1946, Apr 18: Simpson, June Rose (#109)

1946, Apr 24: Baby Boy (#158)

1946, Apr 25: Wolfe, Lorna Rosetta (#119)

1946, May 21: Baby Boy (#170)

1946, Aug 18: Baby Girl (#184)

When the Ideal Maternity Home was finally closed in August 1946, there were reportedly still more than one hundred babies there, who would have been placed with other agencies within the province of Nova Scotia and possibly New Brunswick. Although not adopted from the Ideal Maternity Home, other adoptees adopted in Nova Scotia could still have been babies from the Home, and quite possibly their place of birth could have been registered as "East Chester, Lunenburg County."

If there is a name or date that is familiar to you on this "Search List," or if you were born at the Ideal Maternity Home, or searching for someone who was born there, you can contact Bob Hartlen (the author), by writing to:

Survivors and Friends of the Ideal Maternity Home

294 Radcliffe Drive, Suite 415

Halifax, Nova Scotia, Canada B3S 1E8

Adoption Search
Resources and Contacts

$$\boxed{\textbf{A P P E N D I X} \quad \textbf{V}}$$

Information for New Searchers

It is likely that records under your birth name are not sealed, and are available, providing you know your birth name. Birth names can sometimes be provided by family members, or obtained from old records or documents, etc. If you know your birth name, write to:

Department of Health, Birth Records
1723 Hollis Street, Box 157
Halifax, Nova Scotia
B3J 2M9

The Department will send a form to be filled out and a fee schedule. You will be required to give some information that you likely will not know, such as your mother's maiden name, and your father's name. Provide as much information as you can. If you have none to give, try the following approach:

Give your mother's maiden name as your last name at birth (if known). Where the father's name is requested, indicate "not married," even if you think otherwise. Where the mother's given name is requested, use a name that was common at the Home, such as Rose, or the name of a saint, such as Mary or Anne. With luck, something may match, or you may receive a "request for further information."

The office of Birth Records is aware of the Ideal Maternity Home and is willing to be flexible, especially if no sealed adoption records are involved. If all else fails, write directly to the Director, stating your connection with the Home. You may receive the short form or "wallet" birth certificate, which could confirm or deny your assumptions. What you are really after is the long-form birth certificate, which will give your birth mother's name and place of birth. (In some cases, the birth father's name may be included if it was provided by the mother.) This is a starting point for searching via your mother's family.

Unfortunately, you have to have the information on the "short form" to get the "long form." You will also need an "acceptable" reason for applying for the long form. Acceptable reasons include passport application (under some circumstances), or a work permit application for either the U.S. or Great Britain. Get advice before applying, or get someone to write a general letter of enquiry if you don't want to identify yourself. Again, if all else fails, write to the Director and plead your case.

Note the difference in wording of replies from the Department. "Incomplete match," with a request for further information, is better than "no record of your birth." Use your birth name (if known) when writing to the Department, and use a post office box to ensure you receive your reply (or tell the local post office that you are using that name). On applications, women should use their birth name as their maiden name, and their adoptive name as their married name. If you do not know your birth name, but know you were born at the Home, and providing you were not adopted in Nova Scotia, you can claim to have no records (or proof) of your adoption in any other jurisdiction. You should offer some proof that you were born at the Ideal Maternity Home. Write directly to the Minister of Social Services, and request a search of records to match a birth date from the Home. This is a long shot, but if only one birth is recorded for that date, you can at least begin pushing for disclosure or a passive disclosure.

Adoption Information Act

Nova Scotia's new Adoption Information Act establishes a balance between people's right to privacy and the opportunity for contact between an adopted person and their birth family. The Act has created a new active registry to help people search for members of their birth families. Identifying information will be exchanged only if both parties consent.

Adoption Information on File

The basic record for any adoption consists of legal documents and background information. Recently, there has been a general improvement in the type and amount of information recorded. In the past, records were not as complete and there may be little information available on a particular adoption.

Identifying and Non-Identifying Information

"Identifying information" is information that will likely reveal the identity of another person involved in the adoption. Under the Act, identifying information includes a person's name, birth date, residence, or occupation. "Non-identifying information" may include medical history, physical description, interests, and level of education.

Who can obtain Non-Identifying Information?

You can obtain non-identifying information about an adoption you were involved in if you are: an adopted person nineteen or older; an adopted person under nineteen with the written consent of your adoptive parents; a birth parent; or a birth sibling or birth relative nineteen or older, with the written consent of the birth parent (some exceptions apply).

Who can obtain Identifying Information?

To obtain identifying information, both you and the person you are looking for need to be nineteen years or older. You can request identifying information if you are an adopted person, a birth parent, or a birth sibling with the written consent of your birth parent (some exceptions apply). Adopted persons can also request information about siblings who were placed for adoption in other families. Under most circumstances, identifying information will not be released without the consent of the person being identified.

What if they can't be located?

If the Adoption Disclosure Services Program staff cannot locate the person you are seeking, you will be advised of the steps that were taken. Identifying information cannot be released.

What happens to the Passive Adoption Register?

The Department of Community Services will continue to maintain the Passive Adoption Register. The Register contains the names of all the people who registered before the Adoption Information Act, as well as those who register after January 1, 1997.

If I am already in the Register, do I have to register again?

If you want the Adoption Disclosure Unit to conduct a search, you need to apply again. Searches will be conducted on a first-come, first-served basis. Priority will be given to medical emergencies and cases where the birth parents are over sixty-five years of age. If you wish only to remain on the Passive Adoption Register, there is no need to reapply.

Will there be a charge?

Yes. A fee schedule is included in the application form. Under certain conditions the fee may be reduced.

The First Step

The first step in obtaining information is to register with the Passive Adoption Register. This will record you as someone who wants contact with another person involved in the adoption. Registering will also provide you with all non-identifying information that is available from your record. Once you have registered, the Adoption Disclosure Services Program staff will check for a match. If both parties have registered as wanting contact, a social worker can help you to arrange contact.

The Search

If the other person has not registered, the staff will search for him or her on your behalf. The search is carried out in the strictest confidence to protect the privacy of the person you are seeking. If the person is located, he or she will be asked if he or she consents to contact. If the person objects to contact for any reason, identifying information will not be released. He or she will be asked to provide updated non-identifying information for you. If the person you are seeking has died, identifying information will be released.

If you do not want to be contacted

If you do not want to be contacted, you can formally register your wish by writing the Adoption Disclosure Services Program.

Appeals

All appeals can be made by writing to the Chair of the Appeals Committee c/o the address listed below.

How to register

Write to:

Adoption Disclosure Service Program

Department of Community Services

PO Box 696

Halifax, Nova Scotia   B3J 2T7

If you have any questions, call: (902) 424-2755

Adoption Disclosure Information

Often when adoptees searching for their birth families learn that the parent they have searched for is deceased, they can continue the search for non-identifying information by providing proof of the death of the parent with a copy of either the obituary, or the death certificate.

The Department of Community Services, Adoption Disclosure, is the department to contact to apply for your complete file.

Legislative References

Bill No. 12 (Government Bill);

4th Session, 56th General Assembly Nova Scotia 45 Elizabeth II, 1996.

An Act to Provide for Adoption Information;

Chapter 3 Acts of 1966 The Honourable James A. Smith, M.D., Minister of Community Services;

Access to Disclosure of Identifying Information:
Section 15 (2a) 15
(1) A birth sibling, with the written consent of a birth parent, may apply to the Director for disclosure of the adoptive name of an adopted person of whom the birth sibling is a birth sibling.
(2) Where (a) the birth parent whose consent is required pursuant to subsection (1) is deceased.

Adoption Resources
Parent Finders–Nova Scotia
PO Box 791
Lower Sackville, Nova Scotia
B4C 3V3
Telephone: 902-864-6654
or 902-435-0287

Parent Finders–National Capitol Region
PO Box 21025
Ottawa, South Postal Outlet
Ottawa, Ontario
K1S 5N1
Telephone: 613-730-8305
Fax: 613-730-0345
Email: pfncr@aol.com
Web site: http://members.aol.com/pfncr

Nova Scotia Department of Community Services
PO Box 696
Halifax, Nova Scotia
B3J 2T7
Email: webcoms@gov.ns.ca

Office of The Premier, Province of Nova Scotia
7th Floor, One Government Place
1700 Granville Street
PO Box 726
Halifax, Nova Scotia
B3J 2T3
Email: premier@gov.ns.ca

Office of the New Democratic Party, Province of Nova Scotia
Roy Bldg., Suite 422
1657 Barrington Street
PO Box 1617
Halifax, Nova Scotia
B3J 2Y3
Email: nsndpcau@fox.nstn.ns.ca

Office of the Progressive Conservative Party, Province of Nova Scotia
Centennial Bldg., Suite 805
1645 Granville Street
PO Box 1617
Halifax, Nova Scotia
B3J 2Y3
Email: pccaucus@fox.nstn.ns.ca